Idle Thoughts Writer

Reflections on life and the creative process

by

Thomas Hocknell

'It is always the best policy to tell the truth, unless of course you are an exceptionally good liar.'

'Nothing is easier to write than scenery; nothing more difficult and unnecessary to read.'

Jerome K Jerome

Also by Thomas Hocknell

The Life Assistance Agency

Unfinished Business

The beginning.

I can't recall why I decided to be a writer. It's hardly a sensible decision; it is a well-trodden path littered with drunkards and burned-out husks of hopes. And manuscripts. Enough to wallpaper hallways to their vanishing point. Sorry, this was intended to be inspirational. You still with me? As a child I was fortunate enough to have never met a writer. Perhaps it might have helped in putting me off for life.

We lived on a hill in what was then agricultural Kent, where Chelsea tractors have now replaced actual tractors. My mother tended an allotment, my sister and I, and various Springer Spaniels, while my father walked two miles down the lane to get a lift into the nearest town that held a weekly cattle market and closed its shops on Wednesday afternoons. From there he used to catch the train up to London and returned twelve hours later with smells from another world collected in the wool of his pinstripe suit. I'd sniff his legs as I hugged him when he came in the door, barely in time for bedtime stories, and find the lingering odour of soot and brake dust, Chinatown and diesel taxis.

The most exciting event of the week was the arrival of the mobile library, where we would borrow *Asterix* and *TinTin* books, *the Famous Five* and *Just William*. All I wanted to be was a soldier, or a farmer. It would never have crossed my mind to be a social worker, or writer, as I had no idea what they were, and were unlikely to require equipment such as a L1A1 self-loading rifle, or a John Deere 710 muck spreader, mind you, during my sixteen years of public service as a social worker I often wished it had.

My sister and I had a childhood as uneventful as childhoods should be, so long as you ignore the spectre of all-out nuclear war looming over the bucolic landscape like a disaster movie. I recall the time that an early warning nuclear attack-warning siren was installed in 1983. I hated the idea that I might spend three minutes pondering which toys to clutch before my imminent

1

vaporisation in a two-mile wide fireball, while my parents presumably screamed in terror, or prayed; maybe they are the same thing. Even as a boy I knew our cluster of cottages and houses skirting what had once been a logger's track was not a target of particular strategic importance, the most that happened there was losing a spaniel down a badger set. Yet I knew that the end of my bed was 22 miles from central London, which *was* a target. Whatever happened to a fireball and its fallout 20 miles away was something my imagination could too easily imagine. Even as an eleven-year-old I knew I'd rather dispense with the three-minute warning and just be done with it. Sometimes you want the element of surprise, particularly when it comes to incoming nuclear warheads. Although, in hindsight, perhaps I simply disliked the invasion of a wider world. The early-warning siren installation coincided with the first pop song I recall hearing. It set the bar high. I'll never forget first hearing the solemn opening of Two Tribes by Frankie Goes To Hollywood: *When you hear the air attack warning, you and your family must take cover...* It was more of a symphonic nightmare via Trevor Horn's Sarm West studio than a pop song; although nightmares are seldom sound tracked by impossibly well varnished synth lines and a bassline more purposeful than lava.

No one else remembers the siren: a tall pole topped by its klaxon; it was surreptitiously taken away when no one was looking. But I do. We graffiti-ed our childish dislike all over it, as though silver spray paint might somehow swing the delicate cold war balance in our favour and save the world. I'm unsure this counted as writing, so does little to explain my future career choice, but maybe, if you look carefully enough, you can trace those childhood threads that lead to the clothes of adulthood.

My sister and I, Barry and his brother Chris, used to visit a residential care home in the woods. When I say *in* the woods it did of course have a long curving driveway, through 20foot high laurel and rhododendrons, but we used the 'secret' route, through thick beech woods and long-abandoned logging tracks, up vague hollow-ways and deer paths. We'd emerge from the tree line and

2

cross the lawn, much to the delight of the mentally handicapped adults, as they were then known. They had learning difficulties and Down Syndrome, but we didn't see any of that, we were children, and in some ways so were they. We used to help out at their mealtimes, explore the grounds, and the basement where there was inexplicably a ghost train, or sit with them in the conservatory. A few years ago, I took my four-year old swimming near to where I grew up, and there they all were, in the public pool, endlessly delighting themselves by showing my son how adept they were at diving, while he giggled at such giant kids. It took me back; there may have been a tear, but I was in a pool, so no one noticed; it is the next best thing to crying in the rain.

Write what you know, they say. These days deviating from that advice can result in the sort of Twitter pile-on better described as a public thunder-fuck. It would appear that characters failing to originate from your own immediate culture now risks appropriation, which is a micro-aggression at best. The publishing houses are primed for this. Perhaps there is such a thing as bad publicity. So, yes, write about what you know and nothing else. The only natural conclusion of which is that every work of fiction is required to be autobiographical. In these fragile hands then fiction will be dead before we can say 'it's all made up, it's fun, it's stories. It's why a biographical book on my time as a social worker was considered with exciting levels of seriousness by a major publishing house. There was nothing to make up, apart from the bits I had forgotten.

You might have thought that I'd have thrown myself at the adult world with the confidence that a Desmond (2:2) in Psychology (in the Community) affords, and you'd be correct. I felt like one of those women spinning on a rotating wall at the mercy of a circus knife thrower; it was hard to discern which way was up. Due to falling in with suspect friends I paid too little attention to future plans. Our common ground was playing Mario Kart and puffing spliffs. My first alert to the damaging effects of cannabis was hearing that Tim, a Geordie pal, had been rumoured

3

to have climbed onto the Newcastle Town Hall, requiring to be talked down by armed police following a visit home; a trip which can only be assumed did not go to plan. I'm unsure how off-script you can go from the popular image of cannabis' relaxing properties, but this set the bar high. None of us skinned up with quite the same enthusiasm after that. It was the time of a life when weekend raves commandeered the weekdays, as the comedown from the last merged with the anticipation of the next.

Following a stint as singles buyer in Ealing HMV, which to this day remains a career highlight, I fell into I.T. recruitment. I suspect everyone enters recruitment under similar circumstances. There's no Fisher Price Recruitment consultant playset, consisting of headset, level-headed cockiness and a hangover. It certainly never came up in my career profiling at school, which had pointed to professional dog walker or customer services. Instead, we were paid in cash to turn up for work at 6pm, an ideal start time for spliff-heads, and call up software developers to ask if they might be available for work, whatever that was. I recall our admiration for the company's owner driving a Ford Probe, although in hindsight it had the body shape of a Capri left out in the sun and a name better suited to a sex toy.

What began as a happy convenience led to several jobs in I.T. recruitment. It was here that I spent my time sending poetry to girls in the hopeful exchange of a snog. A friend recently sent me some of them via Facebook. They were not terrible. I mean they were hardly publishable; they were the words of a young man finding hope of snogs in the shapes of clouds. They caught the moment more effectively than they caught the girl, but if twenty-somethings can't utilise poetry as part of a doomed courting process then the world deserves to be over in less than three-minutes. The world spins into new cycles, but some things never change. Actually, most things never really change, they just get a respray or reboot.

Why write?

I write because I don't know what I think until I read what I say. – 'Flannery O'Connor.

You might be questioning the usefulness of a book on writing by an author without a Sunday Times best seller to his name, at least not one he has written. Well, it's because not being a best-seller is the most frequently flown writing trip for most writers. Despite all the inspirational quotes and positive affirmations, you probably won't get published. And if you do then you are unlikely to sell enough to earn a living. That's the hard stuff out the way. So, rather than a tour of Business Class, this book traipses through Economy. It picks through the rejection slips and tattered tenth drafts. This might be the lesser reported experience, yet it's the one which the majority of writers negotiate.

It's all very well reading about success and self-worth accrued by a novel smashing sales figures and its author colliding with the trophy table at award ceremonies, but how about all those other books and their authors? Of course, you are aiming for the top, but statistically the chances are that you will miss by the sort of margin better suited to measure interstellar space distances. But so what? It's still a life. An underselling novel, which is all of them, might not secure you a weekly column in the broadsheets, but it remains you facing yourself. It is still a blank page staring down your hunting instincts for that illusive chameleon called inspiration; it might be paisley on plaid, but your art lies in there somewhere.

This book considers the highs and the lows, definitely the lows. It peers over the fence of creativity and reports back what really happens when your dreams come true. And when they collapse like scaffolding in an earthquake. It records the experience of having your novel published and what follows. It traces the shift from dreams to reality and how we can learn to live with them both, even if they fit together with the camaraderie of a mongoose and cobra.

A rather gloomy piece of recent research shows that 1 in 10 people have never read a novel, which obviously means that 1 in 10 people are fuckwits, but that doesn't change the fact that writing novel sometimes feels like perfecting the steam engine at the advent of the internal combustion engine. Novels belong to a distant age, displaced by TV boxsets and keeping up with What's App groups admin. All books are good for is shelfies. Until you spy a promising book review in the newspaper, and discover you want to be a part of something that doesn't require recharging its battery and instead recharges yours.

There comes a time when a writer asks themselves why am I writing? It's an obvious question, until you ask it. George Orwell in his essay of the same name declared that when he sat down to write a book, he avoided saying 'I am going to produce a work of art'. This is sound advice. The story may unfurl as you chuck it at the empty page, but it will struggle to find life if too entangled in verbosity and loquacity. A novel must climb to its elevation; not find itself born teetering upon the summit of its own self-regarding pedestal. I'm writing this book in the hope it will become a cult classic. That sentence has destroyed any minuscule chance it ever had of becoming so. No one writes a cult classic. They write a book that becomes a classic, often through nothing but serendipity – alongside immaculate writing of course.

Like root canal work, there's never an ideal time for questioning the spark underpinning a desire to write. If writing is for fun, a distraction from your commute, or a challenge amidst the flurry of new year resolutions guided by the misnomer that everyone has a novel in them, then all is good, but if you aim to get published, then perhaps it is important to ask yourself why. For some people with a novel in them it is because they

6

swallowed it. For others the best place for it is to stay in them, but if you don't get that one out of the way you risk failing to clear the tubes for the next one.

Of course, the question why do I write? is the soul-exploring enquiry that many writers scratch and scribble away to avoid. It might have been easier to answer when I started writing. I was sixteen. And although that was only the lyrics to New Order's *True Faith*, which I had copied out and pinned to my wall, a girl asked if I had written the words, and I said yes. She was impressed; we didn't kiss, but I saw the potential in the written word. I just needed words of my own. Where were they to be found?

Let's face it, if you are unlikely to be chosen for football sides, then why not write about where that leaves you. The touchlines are an interesting place if you stand there shivering for long enough. If you're never going to get laid by scoring a goal, then perhaps you might by writing lyrics and pinning them to a wall; even if they're not yours. Thus, perhaps my decision to write a novel might be traced back to an age when I lacked legal responsibility to drive a car or vote, yet I chose it to define myself. I've been nailed to the mast ever since. And I guess living according to the whims of an adolescent boy means I should be grateful that I've not spent my adulthood wrapping souped-up hatchbacks around trees and completing *Street Fighter 2* using nothing but Edmond Honda's hundred-hand slap.

These days when I say I'm working on a novel it sounds alarmingly like I'm ducking out of real life, wearing pyjamas while eating flapjacks in bed, and surfing Wikipedia like it's going to get me somewhere. This might well be what I am doing, but it's best not admit it. You soon recover from the excitement of starting a novel, and it's definitely advisable not to ever announce it.

It often seems as though the best method to vindicate writing is to get published; to be schmoozed by literary agents and publishing houses. After all, published writers obviously wake up with their agent giving them a foot massage, before presenting sales figures that glow in the dark. These are celebrated by a liquid lunch and free taxi rides to exciting West End clubs and room service and the double-glazed blur of a hotel hangover. I can see why people self-publish; it is the fast track to being considered a writer whilst avoiding the fattening lunches.

Anyway, the biggest decision doesn't really involve writing a novel, but whether to mention that you're writing one. You might consider it clever to announce your literary aspirations, but the casual bystander sees it as putting up a shelf and will spend the next ten years asking how it is holding up. A lot can happen in ten years. I mean a lot. You can't even recall the back of your hands from ten years ago. The end to your book can mismatch the start and your author photo belongs to another fashion epoch. I've lost so many agents that it looks deliberately careless, and during more drafts than I would have believed possible I have deleted more words than I've written. I have had the scent for something not yet seen, only to lose it in the fog-heavy undergrowth and the bleary years of early parenthood. You need an iron-grip on your idea. You need grit and the sort of determination to span gorges with bridges that you can safely drive cars across.

It's not in keeping with positive affirmations of creative writing on the Twittersphere but it can be toxic positivity. We sometimes have to engage with the real facts of life: the negativity and doubt and our limitations. Failing to get published is a life challenge and provokes consideration of whether it is time to give up. It might mean abandoning the fantasies and ambitions that have grown to define you, but it might also result in growing up. I've used the fantasy of becoming a published writer to help deal with crap jobs, crazy girlfriends and sodden holidays, yet perhaps it's healthier to live with what you are, not what you wish to be. Following your dreams is all well and good, but last night I dreamt I was a human hotdog, which isn't going to get me anywhere, unless a local fast-food joint needs a new mascot.

When I've mentioned that I might stop writing, well-intentioned people have told me 'you can't do that', like they have investment in me deluding myself. And you know what? They're right. This game isn't about winning, nauseatingly it is about taking part. And after all, apart from Lollypop ladies, and Iron Man, there are few things with their heart in a better place than well-intended platitudes. And nothing alerts you to how bad things have got than when someone slings you a phrase so stripped of meaning that you both have to check something was actually said. It's like waking up to find your partner has left you and being told there's plenty more fish in the sea, when in fact there's so few fish left in the sea that seagulls prefer chips, or attacking small dogs inland, than going fishing.

Sadly, platitudes fall flat when you've spent half an hour losing the ability to spell entanglement; never write yourself into a corner that you can't spell your way out of. It is not just pursuing your dreams, it's stuff like 'be the person you want to meet', which would entail me permanently dishing out invites to a movie premier deck party on a 200ft Sun seeker yacht in Cannes while dressed as the man from Delmonte who's recently hit the service bell calling for exactly what he wants.

However, as anyone who has waited 50 minutes for the P4 bus to Brixton without a book to read will know, good things come to those who wait. It's not rocket science, which is applicable even to rocket science itself these days, while 'only the good die young' surely means that anyone over 42 (that's young right?) is a complete wanker. This is absolutely true, until you reach 42, at which point you see with absolute clarity that it's the other way around. And frankly, unless the proof in the pudding is a large advance cheque then I'm sending it back to the kitchen. As to 'everything will be ok', well, unless you ignore that we're all going to die, this works perfectly.

They also declare that it's the trying that counts, but this isn't rugby, there needs to be justification for all the effort. Sitting studiously staring at I-Tunes or Spotify compiling playlists is undeniably fun, it does not make you a writer. What does make you a writer is being alone and overcoming the internal critic whispering that it's all a waste of time. Perhaps it is, but be careful, hold in mind that doing one thing means you're not doing another, whether it be child rearing, break-dancing or studying, so you have to ask yourself: when is it time to give up childhood dreams? The answer is:

'If it fails, admit it frankly and try another. But above all, try something.' – Franklin D. Roosevelt.

Finding time to write.

Time flies like an arrow; fruit flies like a banana.
— Anthony G. Oettinger

Well, if there was ever irrefutable evidence for Be careful what you wish for, then Lockdown is it. Who doesn't want to spend every day at home instead of going into work? Erm, 'Us' screams a shrill nation having changed their opinion on this long-held view overnight and having given up trying are now neck-deep in laundry and online shopping packaging.

How IS it going? The country is brimming with writers and creatives enjoying everything they ever wanted: time on their hands. No more crying into the soup that life gets in the way of creativity. But now there's no life to write about, unless you're a writer of pandemic apocalypses; the market of which is about to be saturated. It transpires that writers need life to get in the way or there's nothing to escape from. Lockdown has broken society and dragged all concept of time beneath the waves with it.

It started so well. Yay, it's a holiday at home! Initially, and when I say initially, I mean for the first three minutes, lockdown seemed like the best thing since colour television. All those things you meant to do could finally be achieved, like watching WW2 movies during the day, spending time in the garden, indulging proper hour-long tea breaks, (cough), I mean learn Spanish, practice magic tricks, paint the house, refine arguments against chlorinated chicken, etc. But before you could say 'inevitable blanket bombing of homemade sourdough bread across all social media platforms' the reality of lockdown kicked in like an injured moose at a final-year-ceramics show and ruined everything.

11

Somehow, the more time there is the less gets done. A groom can still arrive on time for his wedding if he's overslept on the overnight sleeper to Carlisle whilst wearing a sequined tutu and L-plate but give him a fortnight and he'll still be deliberating his sartorial choice of tie as he walks down the aisle. Meanwhile, during this time of coronavirus, the main activity of the day appears to be forwarding gifs from one WhatsApp group you have no idea why you're a member of, to another.

The lockdown even temporally cured FOMO, everyone was at home doing the laundry, but then Zoom arrived - a kind of also-ran conferencing app that spent most of 2020 upgrading its 2022 Christmas party from Basingstoke's Harvester restaurant to a fortnight all-in trip to the Maldives. Now there's always some Zoom party you've not been invited to. Although you're not missing much, it basically involves waiting your turn to say something, which by the time the opportunity arrives your snappy comment is irrelevant, or someone else has already said. You may as well send retorts by post. If the lighting is poor you appear to be a hostage chained to a radiator, and the only subject is what you have all watched recently on TV.

So, in between bulletins on world leaders not really knowing what the fuck to do, while their economies tank in the background like it's 1928, and medics sign off any death by respiratory disease as Covid19, Lockdown provided the finest opportunity to feel guilty for not writing since the Christmas holidays. It has long been claimed that creativity is discovering your inner child, although the lockdown reveals the truth. Parents have been uncovering that the magical advice of being in touch with your inner child doesn't actually involve fearlessly inventive playfulness, but hysterical tantrums when asked to do anything, such as going to a park, and not eating the same thing every single day.

Writing needs inspiration, which is thin on the ground, unless you count TV boxsets, and no one needs a thinly disguised retread of *Breaking Bad*, although *Ozark* somehow successfully achieves this by transferring the concept of continual firefighting during the worst day ever to the verdant Missouri via accountancy. It's a greener Breaking Bad, but perhaps not in the way environmentalists might prefer. If your creative juices are more frozen than penguin slippers worry not, take inspiration where you can.

The boom in TV is an opportunity for writers to point well-sharpened pencils in the direction of a screenplay. Adapting from an already written book makes things easier as it provides an established roadmap. Some writers already have this when writing novels, but like the sun it is best not to look at them directly; it hurts. Of course, a TV pilot episode might be the last desperate attempt to wring something from an idea that didn't sell as a novel. It's basically tilting the fridge on one side to decant remains of milk spilt in the door shelf. Yet, there might be enough to make milkshake.

As with any writing a screenplay is never finished. Every read through finds minutiae changes until it's tighter than a damp military beret. On the fifth read-through for my recent script the height of the fireplace in scene 34 was lowered an inch, the car was parked neater to the curb, and the removed comma was replaced in a bar scene so noisy that when filmed no one will hear the speech, much less the punctuation. However, what's great is the collaboration. Writing *with* someone is a revelation. It means that both parties can take credit for the best lines, regardless as to whether they wrote them, and disown any poor writing as responsibility of the other person. It's perfect. And with the raising demand in TV shows what better time to be writing one. At least that's the theory.

How easy is it to be alone?

We're born alone, we live alone, we die alone. Only through our love and friendship can we create the illusion for the moment that we're not alone. Orson Welles

We all crave and seek solitariness, yet what happens when we find it and are alone, particularly if there are no Pringles in the house? I guess it provides opportunity to do all those jobs you don't have time for, such as sitting down.

If you put a stethoscope to the wall of most family homes you might hear the echo of people asking if anyone has seen their bloody slippers, or pleading to 'Give me some space', but what happens when you actually get it. When you have more time than you know what to do with? What did we do before Lockdowns or holidays?

Being alone is a lonely business. I've avoided it for most of my life and filled it with the conversation of characters in fictional situations far more interesting than my own, or stroking vinyl records with the delicacy generally reserved for pedigree cats. Being alone does strange things to people. Humans are not built for it. We are social. We congregate and we mill about; safety in numbers, I guess. Too much solitariness means too much time to think, and I'm pretty certain there's a direct correlation between spending too much time alone and believing that the moon landings were a hoax. One of the silent killers isn't a ninja stalking the shadows, but loneliness. I saw that as a social worker; service users had drifted so far from the herd there was no getting back.

We all know of Neil Armstrong and Buzz Aldrin, but it's Michael Collins who is of most interest. He was the most solitary man there has ever been. He was the third astronaut in Apollo 11 and did not walk on the moon. He remained in the command module which drifted behind the moon cutting off his communication with Earth for 47 minutes of absolute silence –

the furthest a man has ever been from earth. He wrote: 'I am alone now, truly alone, and absolutely isolated from any known life. I am it. If a count were taken, the score would be three billion plus two over on the other side of the moon, and one plus God knows what on this side.' He was on the dark side of moon, which hung between him and all that he knew.

I'm certain that Collins speaks for writers staring at the blank page everywhere. I wonder if he actually had the greater spiritual experience than the two men desperate not to fluff their lines as they touched down on the lunar surface. In fact, it's almost possible to feel sorry for the astronauts of Apollo 11, I mean having my second novel *Unfinished Business* published, was rewarding, but it's nothing compared to pressing a button to ignite 27 tonnes of rocket fuel per second sitting beneath your driving seat. It's satisfying to write a neat line of prose, but I'm unsure it provides that level of thrilling propulsion, unless I've been doing it wrong. And where can your life go after that? Even the invention of TV remote controls must have left the NASA astronauts cold. And I struggle to believe a Honda Prius has the level of oomph Armstrong, Aldrin and Collins had grown accustomed to. Mind you, there were given free Ford Mustangs, which might have scratched the itch for a while.

Books are perfect for being alone because it gives you something to do with your hands. It looks purposeful and cool and justifies the odd chuckle of laughter. Something else that clearly relieves people of loneliness is their phones. Where people used to nervously tap out a cigarette and request a light, they now fiddle with their phones. It's probably a step up from that mistaken pubescent idea that flicking open a Zippo lighter increases your attractiveness to the opposite sex, but ironically phone-fiddling prevents face-to-face interaction because it makes you look busy; whereas you can disturb someone reading a book, so long as you approach with care.

But solitariness is something we decline to discuss. Being alone is an important part of self-growth and even idealised, yet is so challenging we seldom do it, unless it is forced upon us by circumstance; now commonly referred to as social distancing. Loneliness is gym-fit FOMO on steroids. It's the sense of forever falling with no impact in sight.

So, to help with appearing particularly purposeful while alone, here are the 20 rules of writing fiction:

The 20 Rules of Writing Fiction

It has to be 20. This is actually another rule. I've already screwed up. The first rule is...

1 To get published. No one gives a flying toot what your rules are until you have proven they work. However, if you are published then you probably didn't even follow any rules, apart from the ones you were making up as you went along, such as joining sentences together, screaming repeatedly, while looking to down tools with the speed of a market stall in the rain at the slightest excuse.

2 Do not stare at your partner, spouse, friend while they are reading the most recent draft of your novel. It will make them sympathise with how a can of dog meat feels as it is opened on the kitchen top. Besides, you're bound to realise that you've printed off the wrong draft for them, so you won't be listening anyway. Several of my ex-girlfriends grew so adept at proof reading that it now features on their CV and dating profile.

3 Once you are published you can pretend you followed some alchemical rules, instead of applying fluke, tenacity, and editing the living fuck out of every word.

4 Like parenting always recommend things you should be doing, not what you are actually doing. Do as I say, not do, basically.

5 Do not think about plot holes during sex. In fact, if you're getting sex give up writing. The whole point of writing is to get laid. You're done (not prematurely).

6 If you're stuck, just bang out some new rules; if nothing else it might create the illusion that you're writing, particularly when in public.

17

7 Always edit drunk, for some reason written bullshit tolerance is reduced by booze, even your own. Weirdly beer is more forgiving of appearance (unless it's the nightclub lighting) than it is grammar. If you don't drink then any sort of altered state will do, whether it's post yoga, or smashed on overly buttered crumpets.

8 Pinning a plot down is like wrestling control of a water hose at full velocity; someone's going to get hurt, but at least the garden gets watered.

9 Another rule is not to waste time writing down rules of writing; it means you're avoiding real work, which is of course the point of writing, but that's one remove too far. Be unafraid to make up rules that suit your mood, such as always write in a bed of biscuit crumbs, or in a bad mood.

10 It is somewhat late in this list for this one but avoid other people's rules. It implies they know what they're doing (which they probably don't) and leaves you feeling inadequate.

11 Throw away notebooks of ideas – you'll never read them. Someone else could find them and base a bestselling novel/film adaptation on your thoughts and you still wouldn't recognise them as yours. Maybe sell just them...

12 'Don't tell me the moon is shining; show me the glint of light on broken glass reports Anton Chekhov. This is advice of the sort writers invent seconds after having brilliantly described the glint of light on broken glass but will be eventually edited out of their novel by their publisher.

13 If no publisher thinks you're worth publishing then self-publish. It can't be worse than anything else out there, with their amateurish fonts Indian firework manufacturers would find too garish. Only if your novel reads less well than one featuring a cat as protagonist, with the spelling of a hasty tweet, should you not self-publish.

14 The most important aspect of writing is how it sounds. Always read out loud. Ensure 'You looked great leaving the house' doesn't read as 'you looked great because you left the house.'

15. Capture the gaps. (This made a lot of sense when I first wrote it. I still stand by it, even if I'm uncertain what it is I meant.)

16 You need to write so you can see your story. The best way to judge the camber of a floor is to roll a marble across it. You can't do this until you've built the floor.

17 Learn to count. To 17 helps. Writers are obsessed with word count, and 17 is the average number of words written before Facebook/blog/Twitter is checked since last time.

18 Editing is like decluttering. You can move books and CDs around the elephant in the room, but until it's gone you can't see clearly.

19' To be an artist means never to avert one's eyes 'wrote Japanese film director Akira Kurosawa, and he's right. Writing does not just concern staring into the light but staring light into the dark.

20 Be careful what you agree to. There are too many musicians and writers wishing they had read the contract, instead being so flush with the thrill of being offered a deal that they masterfully sign over all rights, even to their own name. When you pull into the destination you dreamed of do not buy a coffee at the first café you see. Walk around. Take it on. Breathe.

What makes a writer …?

It's none of their business that you have to learn to write. Let them think you were born that way. Ernest Hemingway.

There is a long-standing belief that writers are respected. Admittedly not by the spouse holding a dripping paintbrush and wondering why instead of holding the ladder the writer is googling the highest point of the Andes in the name of research. But, once upon a time, with nothing but a pen as their weapon, writers seized upon life itself and wrestled it into tight-knitted prose for the pleasure of adoring hordes.

I intended to observe the world with a louche and insightful eye beneath the slow purr of ceiling fans from the corners of colonial cafes where the walls are stained with ancient tobacco smoke, political discussion and illicit liaisons, where intrigue hangs permanently in the air. Annoyingly this is not the life of a writer. The life of a writer is spent finding increasingly intricate ways in which to stop checking your Amazon sales rankings, checking mountain heights in the Andes and avoiding arguments on Twitter, which is a bit like wading through a river trying to evade water. Despite this, many people aspire to be a writer.

I still blame JK Rowling. Since her success everyone wants to be an author, as though buying an arable farm and being prepared to stuff a free toy into every packet of your cereal might bring you Kellogg's level of success. Writers are the sort of people enjoying a quick-witted quip that takes two days to write. Or they are simply so anxious about the fleeting, ungraspable core of life that they want to write it down, so they don't lose it. Yet, losing it is a defining part of being a writer, particularly if 'it' is your ability to earn a living.

Writing may not look hard but bracing your shoulder to your dreams and taking the strain is what makes you one. You will find your enemy, the one whom lives within, the one who feels foolish or sad, awkward or tongue-tied. The one who tells you it is all a waste of time, the one who is harder to pin down than the story itself, although it is nothing compared to discovering your closest friends haven't bought your book.

And where do the ideas come from? Oh, writers often murmur with the gentle confidence last seen in hair tonic salesmen of the 1950s that it's all a breeze. Oh, they say, the characters just write the story themselves, in fact I struggle to keep up, the protagonists have so many ideas, they explain, before you punch them hard in the face. What really happens is that characters can present themselves in full voice from little more than a snatch of overheard conversation, from which an entire novel, a lucrative series with TV and film tie-ins and a West End musical beckon, until the character, so seductive in the twilight of possibility of a road trip, immediately falls unconscious in the backseat and refuses to wake up, expecting you to do all the driving. For 90,000 miles.

The most important virtue of a writer is the ability to write, which is obviously hard work. It's far easier to *say* you are a writer as opposed to silently scream at an empty page or Word document until you decide to write a film script instead, which also involves staring at a blank page and wondering if you might be better off writing a novel.

Writing is really an opportunity to avoid becoming too involved in medieval military re-enactments in your middle age, and to justify loitering in supermarket aisles or taking the family on a day trip to Hinkley Point nuclear power station because a character, destined to be deleted in a particularly vicious edit of your novel, loses his house keys there.

I think the most significant thing that makes a writer is the ability to live with the starkness between what you wanted to write and what is actually on the page. There should be a word for the vast lacuna between your hopes and the reality. It's like herbal tea that always smells of rose petals floating on an offshore breeze; but ends up tasting like dishwater. Writing is

21

living with the reality rather than the promise. And to even get close to this you have to trust that Twitter will eat its own tail without your incensed involvement. You need to be inspired by the quiet microclimates of bookshops not online stores, and to simply crack on with writing the book you most want to read. No one else is going to.

How to start writing a novel

Ideas are like rabbits. You get a couple and learn how to handle them, and pretty soon you have a dozen. - John Steinbeck

To be honest I'm unsure of Steinbeck's expertise with trapping rabbits, but I know that catching them without the help of a tenuous Jack Russell is like grasping at smoke. I also know that he wrote one of the best novels I've ever read. *East of Eden* sat on my bookshelf mocking my reluctance to pick it up for so long that my edition would probably turn heads on the used book market. When I finally read it the story floored me like all literature should; to be fair it's a hefty tome, thick with the girth of wisdom and impossibly vivid relationships. But, how do you start work on your own book that might change the course of lives, or at least accompany someone on the 6:20 from Liverpool Street to Norwich for ten minutes before they fall asleep?

The established method in starting any creative pursuit that doesn't involve immediate satisfaction is to delay it. Stick with what stokes you now, not later. This is what dogs do. They chase the stick until they finally slump in their bed to dream of sticks. Writers are not dogs. Writers watch the juicy stick arc into the air, drool, and IGNORE it. When people declare how much they'd like to be a writer they are referring to that alluring type that everyone at the party talks about the following day. The one that gets elegantly drunk, laid and avoids the hangover. Well, that's not how it works.

You start writing a novel like mopping a floor. You turn up, you get the water at a passable temperature and start slopping it around. It's clumsy and inexact, but it gets the floor clean. No one admires a cleaner, yet everyone admires a shiny clean floor. And then, when it's done, if you're a writer, you have to do it again. You don't make a fire with the flare of short-lived newspaper, you need wood; chopped and seasoned. It's boring and systematic. A good fire needs to be prepared twelve months previously.

All writers have been here: the hinterland between the joy of completing a project and the niggling sense that it's time to start another. Life basically becomes a decision between buying a dog or writing a new novel. Mind you a book doesn't plead to be walked or be fed, although it does rest its head on your lap and look up at you expectantly; wondering when you're going to write something. I only ever had the ambition to write one book, I thought that would be enough, but it is strangely addictive.

Unfinished Business was published as a continuation of the Life Assistance Agency's adventure and the challenge of starting a new novel is that having spent three-years focused on one story is to discover there's nothing left to occupy your mind. Most writers emerge blinking from editing into the sunlight hoping that something interesting might happen at their launch party to trigger a new book, although there's only so many stories involving regretting your rash image change, forgetting to eat, and falling over the merchandise after drinking too much. It's like empty nest syndrome when you've spent 18 years shouting at your children to not leave the house without shoes and discovering there's no one left to swear at; and that relinquishing the TV remote happened so long ago that you don't even miss it. What now?

You sit in a cafe where only weeks ago you were contently editing with purpose, to find a hollow lack of focus, and ideas. There is the unmistakable sound of drumming fingers. And not just your own, but the characters. You can hear them mooching moodily around your unconscious like teenagers on a family holiday, wondering when the parents might go out so they can surreptitiously drink the pineapple schnapps smuggled in their hand luggage.

Starting a new novel feels like leaping off a building clutching a rope whilst yelling back at people at the top to attach it to something secure, without ensuring there's anyone up there. It is a thousand punch lines without a joke: it's answers without questions and hats lacking racks. It's as thrilling as it is terrifying.

People often ask writers why they write, (although never Plumbers why they plumb), and when I sit down to start, it soon became evident why I write. It's to spend money. I have written a few lines before I start, but then I'm busy spending all the unlikely royalties on vinyl records before I have even clocked what's happening. Like pulling in a nightclub, it's sometimes unclear what you've got involved with until you get home. I was buying records like a club DJ with an actual crowd eager to hear my latest cuts, as opposed to playing them alone at home. And I was doing no writing. I couldn't even pretend it was research.

Danielle Steele apparently writes for 22 hours a day, which perhaps excuses her books, although you can't deny the commitment, if not to writing then certainly to an industrious self-image. Perhaps she's also a vinyl junkie, although I suspect she can afford to be. Paulo Coelho also states with alarming certainty that writing requires discipline. Mind you, he does wake up at midday and still finds time for an afternoon nap when not working on a book; so, I guess that's all the time then.

It was time to stop mucking about. I visited the Isle of Sheppey in Kent for research, which feels as cut off from the world as you always imagined. There was birdsong and scrap yards, medical research companies and caravan parks rolling out across the hills like net-curtained shoeboxes. There was a Dickins pub with a Reliant Robin dumped in the front garden. Only Fools and Sauces was its tagline. You can imagine on-going high fives celebrating the success of such top-level punning, although the neglected front garden suggested their skills in self-promotion did not stretch to pruning. It reminded me that if you hang around for too long, you'll find a TV series already treading on the themes of your unwritten novel, guaranteeing no agent will touch it.

The five-hour road trip to Sheppey resulted in 500 words being written, which is a good return on mileage and it's hard to buy records at 70mph on the M2. It is this sort of day trip in the name of research that makes writing so worthwhile. It is trips without purpose that often return well on your investment. And there remains a footpath I still want to investigate. I glimpsed my characters walking down it as I left, and I want to see where they were going. Perhaps that is the best place to start. I may not even need to return to find out.

Writing is truly showing yourself; the fear is that how you are then seen is out of your control. The persona is effective, but it's cold. Show yourself to yourself. And the world might be interested too. If not, well, at least you tried; or find another world.

Creating your perfect Writing space

Sheep herds must have been applying for relocation in Chipping Norton when David Cameron installed a traditional shepherd's hut in his garden. The direct impact of writing in a shepherd's hut is yet to be properly investigated, but if Cameron wanted the full experience, he'd be better off sitting on his lawn staring at white shapes eating grass from beneath a waxed poncho for weeks at a time and doing no writing.

Regardless of your politics, it is easy to understand the appeal of a hideaway, particularly if you introduced a referendum that many did not want. Cameron will be writing his memoirs in there, and he can't be expected to do that in his local artisan café, even if populated by the Chipping Norton set walloping him with copies of *the Guardian*.

Beach huts hold similar appeal, with writers justifying borrowing money secured on future royalties to secure the ideal creative environment in which to write the book that will secure the royalties. Ironically, written down that appears even worse as a business plan than when spoken aloud. There are probably stronger grounds for buying a beach hut as a holiday getaway with children, but kids are as conducive to writing as a malfunctioning burglar alarm, albeit with a greater appetite for snacks.

The desire to own a beach hut is timeless; a fantasy shared by 5-year-olds to 80-year-olds alike. They appear like boiled sweets from a distance and serve the same purpose as a garden shed, without being greeted by an avalanche of forgotten rusting gardening equipment every time you open it. They are an escape. It's basically caravanning without the need for a warning triangle, extended wing-mirrors and a mildewed Alpine Sprite 4 dumped on the driveway blocking the view all year round. The sole purpose of beach huts really is to provide somewhere to boil a kettle, when it'd be easier, and far cheaper, to buy one from the

27

local café and drink it on the seawall. Australians see the beach as somewhere to demonstrate physical prowess such as muscle flexing and frisbee; the Brits see it as somewhere to dunk biscuits in hot drinks in cold weather. I know which side I'm on.

The first thing you'll notice is that hut owners spend far less time stripping off for a swim, than they do stripping down wood to treat, varnish and paint. It's never-ending. If you like DIY then buy a beach hut, but if you like sitting around in the sun watching other people work then visit a friend who owns one. If you get bored, you can always admire the passing procession of increasingly complicated mixed breed canines and overhear snippets of conversations as people stroll past. Apart from following the passers-by, the only way to enable more complete eavesdropping is to station friends at regular intervals along the row of huts, but before completing any admin on this you'll hopefully have wondered why the hell you're bothering, instead of brewing another cup of tea that you don't want just because you can.

The crucial life skill when sitting outside a beach hut is to not look too pleased with yourself. This is harder said than done, as beach hut owners achieve new depths of smugness. I've basically become one of those annoying people who look for conversation opportunities, like a boxer eyes gaps in an opponent's defence, to mention owning a hut. I've become one of those who introduces a subject without any grounds whatsoever for doing so, like an actor recently having secured a coveted part. However, I've not done much writing.

One of the joys of a hut, like a houseboat or tent, is that everything is within reach. You never have to go upstairs to look for something that you can't remember when you get there. Mind you, the fact that everything is within reach doesn't mean you shall find it if you neglected to bring it with you in the first place. There's something comforting about close proximity of your belongings; it's like inhabiting a well-kitted out womb.

As to the writing, it's all very well achieving the perfect environment in which to create, but all the best ideas for novels come when you're running for a bus without a pen, which is the sort of creative environment that is a struggle to maintain with any continuity, although is cheaper than a beach hut.

E. B. White, the author of *Charlotte's Web*, used to write at the kitchen table in a busy house, saying he could always go somewhere else, so could never complain. He claimed that a 'writer who waits for ideal conditions under which to work will die without putting a word to paper.' He is bang on. So, where is the best place to write?

Writing in a local café – how much gets done?

Where do writers get their stories? is probably the most common question writers ask themselves after 'why did I bloody start this? 'and 'shall I work from home, or the local cafe? 'Cafes have long been presumed to be full of poets, artists and novelists so it is a non-brainer; until you get there to find it rammed with harassed looking mothers with screaming pre-school offspring and architects 'working from home'. And other bloody writers. You instantly wish you'd gone for that country walk instead. That was before the Covid lockdowns, now the café is closed, or full of masked people lacking half their facial expressions as favoured by bank heist enthusiasts; the world is at gunpoint.

How much work actually gets done at home? Since lockdowns this is a question that more people than ever can honestly answer. I imagine employees requesting to work in the office after six months of sitting in pajamas from the waist down in the sweet spot of a flat that maximises wi-fi connection, whilst avoiding exposure of your interior furnishings. Homes are for returning to, not to be trapped within.

I'm not even sure that much homework gets done at home anymore. Working from home involves sauntering about, achieving little more than moving stuff that may or may not need to be moved from one room to another, and often then back again. It's lots of pacing, generally out of rooms that need things doing in them. I once walked five miles without opening the front door. Homes are best suited for lounging surrounded by books, while the wind throws rain at the windows like sharpened gravel, not for working in.

I was always struck by JK Rowling reporting how writing in a cafe was the hallmark of a breadline writer, when it's actually far easier to write in a cafe than it is at home. There's less distraction, and there's less wandering aimlessly like a near-sighted field mouse searching for its glasses in the cafe.

However, writing regularly in the same public space also has its pitfalls.

It is amazing how much of writing in cafes is actually spent talking to anyone ill-advisably making eye contact. Although, in all honesty, there's a trick to hovering your fingers over a keyboard whilst hoping someone will talk to you. Writing can be a lonely business and if there's one thing writers enjoy doing more than writing it's talking about it. Trust me on this. If they're not talking about it then they are required to start writing it and talking is easier than doing.

Scribbling in public means you will meet other writers. They're the ones sighing loudly at the harassed looking parents continuing to insist on frequenting their old childless haunts as though a screaming one-year-old should not prelude them from anywhere. You can't swing a copy of the Writers '& Artists' Yearbook in a coffee house without hitting scribblers. And generous offers to read others' manuscripts sound like your own voice because they are, until you're spending more time reading their manuscripts than your own.

There is a contentedness associated with working from home, as though eating cold pizza for lunch in your pyjamas is a mark of success, and perhaps it is, but if you stay at home you don't get to chat, and you don't get the stories. And you don't get respect from flat mates or partners. Although admittedly you don't find yourself leaving with more manuscripts than the one you arrived in the café with.

One of the chaps I met in my local cafe was Bob – who yes, used to be builder. For once I am not making this up. He was born in South London in 1929, left school at 14 and followed his father into the building trade. He passed away recently aged 86 shortly before Christmas in Lewisham hospital and it was a pleasure to have known him, and not just because he bought one of my novels despite not having read a book in his life.

Stories were told at his funeral of his many narrow escapes with death that one was almost tempted to knock on the coffin to ensure he had indeed passed. We were told of one occasion when the health and safety wisdom of working on a roof by tying your waist to the nearest chimney stack was challenged by the chimney collapsing. It took Bob down with it. He arrived soot-laden in a fireplace to the shock of the owners.

Before being evacuated to Wales for the Blitz Bob recalled a mobile Anti-Aircraft gun was parked outside his house in west Dulwich. During an air raid it began firing and the noise blew out all the windows in the street; causing more local damage than the Germans ever achieved. He was also narrowly missed when a Nazi fighter bomber strafed Goose Green, killing several school children: one beside him. My father, the same age as Bob, also recalls German aircraft machine gunning a children's playground in Catford as they returned home. There were holes in the washing drying on the lines. You don't get these stories at home.

R.I.P. Robert Hobbs.

The importance of sitting in the corner

So, writers will be familiar with the coffee shop as an important element to the writing process. It's all very well setting up a lovely study at home in which children are banned from singing the theme tune to *Yo-Kai Watch* if you have opportunity, but chances are that instead of writing you'll spend the day enmeshed in the intricacies of telephone banking, or pointlessly rearranging your books in the order that you inaccurately recall buying them in. Leaving the house is a good idea for anyone, particularly writers, who are already predisposed for seeing things that aren't there.

Despite writers appearing as cutting edge as the 1980s robots advertising instant mashed potato (Smash!), it's good for people to see writers at work. It may not hold attention for long, after all, how entertaining is a person frowning, but we do need to publicise our existence. One of the most common responses in people upon discovering that you're a writer, after the initial slack jaw of disbelief, is the question 'are those still going?' You reassure them that books are indeed 'still going' despite a part of you being deeply aware that needing to explain this demonstrates how the battle lines have been redrawn. It's too easy to believe these days that books are simply a bunch of words to wrap eye-catching artwork around.

My local coffee shop has a such a regular clientele that no one needs to order anymore. As in PG Wodehouse novels, customers are known by their regular order: Flat White, English Breakfast, Tight Arse Who Brings His Own Banana, etc. And as any creative knows, the fetish of how and where you write is crucial. The aforementioned Wodehouse invariably wrote with a Pekinese warming his feet and was finished by an early lunch, while Hemingway's prose was soaked in whiskey and manliness and probably started at lunchtime at the earliest following some wood chopping after arm-wrestling the axe from the hands of local lumberjacks.

As a tea drinker in a coffee world, I feel like a cake on a pie stall, but as I'm tapping studiously into my laptop, carefully compiling playlists for future unwritten novels, I feel at home. That is if I'm in a corner. I'm unsure why being cornered is the perfect muse. Sailors had mermaids, and writers seek nice secure corners. It's advisable not to analyse this too closely, but the knowledge that your back is covered is reassuring.

However, you will find yourself in competition for the corner. Sadly, there are only four corners in a room, and there are other writers stained with cowboy-blood; all refusing to sit with their back to the door. I had been hoping for a blue plaque on the window seat corner of my favourite cafe, but another writer has started arriving before me, and I refuse to share a plaque, particularly if he's more successful than me. He always appears too tired to write, so instead sits there looking smug, although he might just be baffled as to where he is; it's hard to tell. I notice he's not confused enough to not reliably arrive before me in order to occupy my table. I vaguely hope he's writing a better novel than I am to justify his commitment to a corner table, but it's not a sincere wish. He's got no excuse not to be. There needs to be some method of measuring the literary ability of customers to ensure the corners get the writers they deserve. I'd suggest this, but who wants competitive writers kicking off, knocking over displays of pain au chocolates and flinging inkwells at one another?

Perhaps writing at home might be preferable. There's less competition and you can occupy any corner you like; the corners are your oyster. Perhaps a more lucrative future than writing best-selling novels might be to subvert the laws of physics and invent rooms with more than four corners to accommodate more writers. It might even be easier than writing a book.

How useful are writing prompts?

'True life is elsewhere. We are not in the world.' Arthur Rimbaud

Anyone without access to a local cafe might assume that writers spend their time posting pictures of finished manuscripts complete with word count on social media. They leave a trail of inspirational hashtags and writing prompts like Hansel and Gretel through the woods.

I have never been a fan of writing prompts. They sound too deliberate, like intending to do shots before you leave the house, instead of spontaneously deciding eight tequilas is a good idea on reaching the pub. To be fair, life is a writing prompt, as anyone who's written a To-Do list will testify. However, I was recently exposed to the most fantastic inspiration for writing at my local B&Q, which I thoroughly recommend. It was unexpected because visits to DIY shops mainly involve forgetting why you went and buying a foot-pedal bin that was on special offer.

These days there are hash tags for everything, although a sweet sense of fresh territory arrives when coining a new one on Instagram and #DIYWritingPrompts was a new one. At least it was yesterday. Imagine being the person who created the first hashtag. The person who first wrote #sandwich probably continues to sell out lecture halls to #rabidfans on six-month rolling national tours with a fully stocked merch stall and struggles to sleep without the sound of #applause ringing her ears.

I did not expect to find writing prompts in B&Q. There's no bloody escape. Paint tester strips can basically outline a novel. It's not 50 shades of grey it's more like 2000 and counting. I'm talking about the names of paints. No, wait, come back. Anyone who's not argued over the merits of Deja Blue (X91) over Blue Grace (X90) hasn't lived. Sadly, you can't simply join them up to create a novel, you do have to fill some of the bits in-between, but there are worm holes, love stories and missed connections amongst the countless hues. I work in a room that can be factually described as bohemian bliss.

I'm still unclear what a writer was doing in a DIY shop. Writers are better suited to describing rooms, or cluttering them up, not decorating them, although this argument is a poor one in the face of a room actually needing to be decorated. I had been hovering around the merits of Refreshment Stand (R2221D) compared to Kernel of Truth (W24B) like a bee in a florist when I was accused of staring into the middle distance. This is a vocational hazard for writers, and initially I was unsure if it was a compliment or not. This uncertainty did not last for long.

From breakdowns on the M1 (B673G) and sex education in schools (D31K). The hues are cues to unwritten thrillers or even self-help books. There's such an oblique wisdom from Farrow and Ball that they could write fortune cookies as a side-line. They have Sulking Room Pink, Red Earth and Blazer, which is basically a sci-fi novel waiting to happen.

So, there I was faced with a thousand unwritten novels when I found the perfect colour for the bedroom ceiling. I could wake up every morning to R139B, or Glowing reviews, as it's also known. This spoke of the future. Why settle for five-star reviews on the Internet when you can bask in the yellowy hue of R139B with little more effort than a ladder and some bleach to get splashes out of the carpet.

How important are Daily Rituals?

I don't count my sit-ups. I only start counting once it starts hurting. Muhammad Ali.

Well, ain't this the big one. Who are the people signing up to the creative life in the hope that a pencil behind your ear or paint on your jeans makes you interesting? The ones that don't make it. They might get laid, but you don't swerve the 9-5 by choosing creativity over corporate life. It's the misconception that many learn the hard way. You have to graft.

The greatest hurdle, and the real break in the clouds of creativity, is the realisation that it takes regular grind like body building or plumbing to be productive as a writer. 500 words only takes half an hour a day, yet over a year that's approximately 182,500 words: the equivalent of two novels. 500 words doesn't sound much, but that's every day, sometimes you might only be oven-firing bricks to build later, but you're still at the desk. It looks easy, but it is not. We're not very good at sitting still.

How d'you find time to write? is the most common response to a writer announcing they are working on a novel. It implies that you have not only discovered some secret stash of time under the stairs, but even more impressively you know what to do with it. Yet, there's always time, you may not necessarily be around to see it all, but it will plod on regardless. Tap in.

Life at its most basic is how you spend your time. Chefs like to literally chop stuff up, while crime writers enjoy chopping stuff up literally. Time can be like porridge or silk, you either have enough, or it runs away from you. Besides, having time to write does not automatically mean you'll do any. In fact, give someone unlimited time and they are likely to achieve sod all, nothing beyond the ability to mumble mañana beneath their breath. As we know, nothing fuels invention like necessity. If you want something done, give it to a busy person.

37

Writing is snatching at moths; occasionally you will kill at first attempt, but generally it's simply clutching at air. This might be why writers like rituals, to tell them that they are writing and not just looking for things that aren't there, rituals provide context, which is crucial in any meaningful life.

Rituals are useful because you know what follows everything else. You sharpen the knife to cut. You hear an ice cream van in the distance and start talking loudly so your children don't. However, unlike carpentry, writing is not 80% preparation. With timber you need the table legs accurate the first time, or you risk ending up with beautifully crafted firewood, whereas with writing you can modify the legs until they become a chair.

An important ritual to establish is what time of day you write best: observe the lulls in the week and aim to use them. You don't need to write all day. Twenty minutes of writing is more productive than a week of good intentions.

Research is the age-old euphemism for procrastination. It can be essential, even if it results in nothing more than developing short-lived expertise in the Meaco DD8L Zambezi dehumidifier, but too often it leads down the google warp hole. Do your writing and then your research. Writing is tapping into your groundwater. Any pause and you might lose the stream (of consciousness). Steinbeck was very precise about this. The flow is all. And if the aircraft you've chosen to fly struggles to glide at 20,000 feet then change the type of plane later, or just research the G-force required to pin you against the wall.

Of course, it's ritualistic to publicly announce completion of your novel, although thankfully not having read one, not yet. Jonathan Franzen has recently said that no one has more than five novels in them, but five celebratory declarations seem inadequate. Predictably the initial declaration is premature. My first announcement garnered enough likes to freeze my Facebook account, but after a rewrite and effectively finishing for the second time, the announcement lost its impact. And so on. Completing a first draft is like winning the 100 metres, before running twenty laps' of 1600 meters afterwards with no one looking.

One of the more encouraging creative rituals is writing in bed, of which George Orwell, Mark Twain, Winston Churchill, and Marcel Proust were all fans of; it sounds cramped, but their writing never was. It's worth engraving those names on your bed's headboard to point at when doubters disturb your creative process, while clarifying that you've not shagged them. The danger is that writing in bed can appear lazy, particularly if you're snoring, at least until you have pointed out the literary greats on your headboard. If you're lying there not writing, then it is advisable to be prepared with the DCR (deep creative repose) argument. Or just tell them to fuck off.

Other suggestions of helpful rituals include a walk without destination. I do this every time I find myself in the aisles of the local supermarket, which I suspect is a method alien to Charles Dickens, whim embraced daily three-hour country walks, or Henry Miller who preferred to wander around Europe trying to get lost. Europe?! Many of us are lucky if we manage a wander into the kitchen without children requesting that we fetch them something. And that was before lockdowns.

Other rituals include Pulitzer Prize winning author John Cheever writing mostly in his underwear, although unless you're going commando most writers tend to do this, and the most effective ritual is probably stringing words together.

Everyone has rituals and writers are no different. Even avoiding habits will find a distinct pattern. It is preferable to emulate Stephen King, who has a cup of tea and sits at his desk with some music and writes six pages every day than it is to copy Murakami who is the sort of writer you wish would decline interviews. His habit is to awake at 4am, work for five or six hours, and then run for seven miles or swim, read a bit and then go to bed at 9pm. I mean come on, some of us have hangovers to endure.

There are rituals everywhere. I have no peculiarities: some carefully curated music and a good window seat, which isn't only so people can see that I am a WRITER but is also a good place to people-watch. Mind you, I'm such a regular at cafes that it might be financially worthwhile for locals to read my books and hit me up for royalties, or a lawsuit. And if your next novel hits the literary world like a bar stool at a chair trade show then you can blame your inspirations for failing to be interesting enough, but if you're canny then your rituals are bullet proof.

10 things successful people do before breakfast.

Have you ever read one of those articles outlining 10 things successful people do before breakfast? The ones you instantly regret starting yet can't finish, as unfettered desire for self-flagellation takes over. These articles are intended to expose your own dawn gloom, as if you needed reminding from a magazine so glossy you can see your own haggard face superimposed over the airbrushed models. I think they're called aspirational magazines, but most people aspire to eat less Gregg's steak bakes and don't need an expensive magazine to remind them.

The main thrust of these pieces is 'do you aspire to have the pizzazz (whatever that is) of Heidi Klum? The inventive streak of Martha Stewart? The $US3.1 billion net worth of Starbucks head honcho Howard Schult? Well, it turns out that waking up a few hours earlier might be the secret. To be honest I'd rather have an extra hour sleep, but that kind of slovenliness is not what thrusted the western world from darkness into the industrial age. The thing is, it's all about the pursuit of wealth, and pizzazz of course. But what's wealth if it can't buy an extra hour in bed?

Everyone is obsessed with money. The Left are obsessed with some people having more than others, while the Right are obsessed with people earning it. Yet there is no time of year like Christmas in the UK to realise how little we actually need. It's not like the 1950s, when a plumbed-in bath was like the arrival of a new civilisation. Folks on their death bed don't wish for more money, but for more time. Money may buy a better quality of life, but so does imagination and appreciation of what you have.

But anyway, apparently, stumbling out of bed, 'grabbing a bad bodega coffee '(whatever the fuck that is) and heading to the office before you have fully grasped whether it's the weekend or not is apparently not only bad for your health, but it's bad for your career.

Productivity coach Jeff Sanders, author of *The 5am Miracle* aims to change these bad habits. He advocates 'easing yourself into the day and using the quiet morning hours to get a head start on work, as well as working on yourself. It's the time of day when you're the most focused, the most energised. Has this man ever actually met any real person in the morning? For some lighting their first cigarette without setting their hair alight is an achievement. And surely what better way than to work on yourself than getting enough sleep so you're not staggering through the day as though you've been shot in the head. He advocates doing 10 things before breakfast. And not one of them appears to include anything a sane person might do. I'm unsure I achieve 10 things before supper but still.

PLAN FOR TOMORROW THE NIGHT BEFORE

To make the most of today, you need to start yesterday. Like ex-president Obama, who sets out his schedule the night before, or at least gets someone else to. This is good advice. I always plan to drink a cup of tea when I wake up.

DRINK LOTS OF WATER

A 2012 study showed that even mild dehydration caused difficulty in concentrating. "The first thing I do, before breakfast, coffee, before working out, is drink four 8-ounce glasses of water to wake my body from the inside out," says Sanders. I can only presume there is a good wi-fi connection in Howard Schultz's toilet.

CHANNEL YOUR INNER BUDDHA

I mean, what??? Sit cross legged humming. It's a lovely idea, but it doesn't get the kids to school with the same efficiency as screaming at them while stalling the car in irritable rush hour traffic.

HIT THE GYM

Morning exercise gives you energy to start the day, but it also gives rise to creativity. I'm not sure being helped out from beneath dumbbells by gym staff is a particularly noble way to start the day, but Vogue editor Anna Wintour plays tennis every day before work. So, there you go. Besides, 'Hit the gym. 'Who actually talks like this?

TURN THINGS UPSIDE DOWN

Yup. This is serious. And if these are the sorts of creative ideas Jeff Sanders is getting as a result of waking up so early perhaps it is advisable that he stays in bed. The tips are becoming increasingly unhinged. He suggests becoming a real-life Batman by donning gravity boots and hanging upside down for 10 minutes a day. 'It sends blood and oxygen rushing to your brain.' Well, I guess it will make it easier for your family to kick you in the head.

The fact that author Dan Brown is an advocate of the technique is hardly encouraging and might explain rather a lot in terms of his prose. However, he has sold a huge number of books, so if there's any pattern here of slamming Dan, it's born from envy. He's a focused writer, and annoyingly that is what makes one.

EMBRACE THE QUIET TIME

Benjamin Franklin spent up to an hour quietly milling around his chambers, reading or writing. It was his way of greeting the day and gathering his thoughts. Now this I can get with, but surely this can happen at any time of day, which is why most writers became writers, to mill around, (cough) I mean crack on with the manuscript.

TACKLE A BIG PROJECT

Basically, Sanders himself attests to this by saying "I wrote my book during the early hours." The only appropriate response to such smugness is to wish he was wearing his gravity boots so you can more easily kick him in the head. For the majority of people activities in the early hours involves foolishly concocted booze formulas.

READ A MOTIVATIONAL BOOK

Everyone needs a cheerleader, Sanders says, and that's fair enough, although I'm less sure wives and girlfriends would approve. However, some sickeningly platitudinal motivational book that only helps the author by selling in its millions, is a less attractive idea. It does however justify writing this book

CLEAR THOSE EMAILS

Take a leaf out of Martha Stewart's book and use the early hours to start sifting through your mail. I admire this, but I seriously question the wisdom of wasting an hour's sleep to go through emails from garden centres and Juno Records confirming the latest record I've ordered that I didn't need.

DO SOMETHING NON WORK-RELATED

Finally, he starts talking sense. Presumably it's finally daybreak and he's in the company of normal people who haven't spent the previous four hours clearing the palette for the day and now need to return to bed. As he says it can't be all work, work, work.

How Important is the opening scene?

'Start as you mean to go on and keep on doing it.' - Scott Wildblood, Proprietor, and lead Assister at the Life Assistance Agency, who is better known for asking other people to do stuff on his behalf and drumming his fingers loudly until they do.

The importance of a novel's killer opening scene in a world of podcasts, impulsive dating, angry fruit games and watching idiotic American sitcoms during your commute is more important than ever. Whatever happened to staring out the window, or reading a book? Well, perhaps the opening chapter failed in its job to secure attention.

It might be necessary to write several opening chapters. I certainly hope so. I tend to write enough to delude myself I'm starting a different book every day. Finding your opening voice in any fiction project can burn the trail where later there is none. However, if it's illusive then it might be best to press on and return to it later. Try to drop the reader into the action. You want them sprawled on the carpet clutching a mysterious business card 60-feet below a skylight surrounded by shards of glass. You want them wondering what just hit them, as though they just opened a box with a boxing glove on a spring.

It can be tempting, when you have a good idea for a chapter, to float around on its possibility for days before wading in. This is a mistake. Strike while the fist is clenched. Strike first and strike hard. No mercy. It's karate, kid. Keep going and discover momentum. You might even find that by writing so many opening chapters you can simply join then together to make a completed novel. I recently sat down to discover my current project as four opening chapters. I looked around to blame the numbnut who had done this, but there was only me to blame.

It is important to spellcheck, so you don't end up talking about the impotence instead of the importance of opening scenes but do it later. As in life, live with the mistakes behind you. Allow the writing to be virile, let it strut and ripple its muscles in the late afternoon pre-cocktails breeze.

Readers don't have the patience, and rightly so, for a two-page descriptive passage leading to eventless autumnal walks through expansive grounds of a Greco-Roman house. We consider the weather later on in this book, but pleasant as the Fall is, unless you're a weather description virtuoso, it's advisable to leave detailing it until you have the reader in a headlock on the canvas. Then they'll read anything you throw at them.

So, how do you get someone's attention once the GREAT cover art has projected the book in their hands? If you can forgive the Union Jack parachute of *The Spy Who Loved Me*, complete with grinding disco funk and moving scenery operated by a boy on work experience, James Bond films have always understood fine first scenes. Some Bond openers were so good that they overshadowed ensuing films, and not just Bond films either, but *all* films. These scenes might have been best left for the finale, but without them no one would have reached the end. This might also be applied to novel writing, hook them in, and leave them wanting more, not regretting pages turning further away from the good bit.

Advice as frequently ignored as that to rinse plates before putting them in a dishwasher is to start the scene half-way through. You want the reader ducking for cover from machine gun fire, or swimming for their life amidst burning aviation wreckage and lifejackets, whilst wishing they'd paid less attention to the duty-free catalogue and more to where the whistle and valve to top-up the life jacket might be found in an emergency.

However, some books are a slow burn. John Williams' *Butcher's Crossing* follows the classic western simmer, before dragging you helplessly into the sort of drama that makes you drop to your knees in gratitude for modern creature comforts and that buffalo hides no longer serve as legal

46

tender. So, it's best to remember that the opening scene doesn't necessarily require action, but it does require intrigue.

So, apart from the autumnal walk, what is going on? The reader will always be asking 'why is the writer telling me this? ' If you can answer, then things might well be working (let's not get too carried away), but if you have less idea of what's going on than a brothel's front lawn then it might be advisable to step away and consider things.

It was the best of times, it was the worst of times . . . like life, let the opening pose questions that the end hopes to answer. You may not even know them yet, but that is the thrill, at least it is if you're a writer. For anyone else it looks as exciting as homework.

Perhaps the best advice is to remember that a story has no beginning or end, so plunge in at the best bit, and then save the really best bit until last. Lastly, if you think writing is hard, then it might be worth considering the advice of folk-style (whatever the hell that is), freestyle wrestler and coach Danny Mack' Dan' Gable and start wrestling. 'Once you have wrestled, everything else in life is easy. 'He says, and let's face it no one's going to contradict him. Take the plunge. And ignore the duty free.

How I wrote my first novel

I started *the Life Assistance Agency* many years before it was picked up. It was initially called the Karma Account, which considered how our deeds might determine our destiny, leading me to consider how hard this must be for people who are immortal, which must become particularly laborious once they find themselves in the 200th year of having seen everything before. The hardest thing about growing old is that eventually there's nothing new; you've seen it all.

Not knowing any immortals to ask, I had to make one up. Or rather I didn't. I forget how I first encountered Dr. Dee, the Elizabethan alchemist from the late 1580s, but I'm glad I did. Not that he is immortal, as far as I know, but he is the closest a historical figure gets to one. He had pursued angels, so it was an easy leap to assume him chasing immortality. If anyone ever has achieved it then Dee is likely to be first in line.

Dee appeared as a good starting point, particularly in the absence of any others. Actually, Damon Albarn and a few other writers were drawn to Dee at a similar time, which initially angered me - hold on, he's my historical figure - I then concluded it was all rather elegant synchronicity, which suggested I was on the right track and would subsequently find myself colliding with success with the ease that gap-year Australians encounter immediate friends, inflatable hammers and vodka jellies.

It's hard to remember the first thing I ever wrote. I recall a story involving my Action Man that was never finished, which is probably for the best. I remember sitting down when I was 21 and asking flat mates to not disturb me, as I scribbled poems that in my mind's eye were part-obscured by curling smoke of Gauloise cigarettes and unrequited love. That the latter was still easier to come by via a local newsagent selling French cigarettes was particularly galling. (Excuse French regional pun). I then tried writing short stories, but made the mistake of simultaneously reading Raymond Carver's, which set the standard too high.

I was drawn to the spirituality of the Romantic poets, who seemed to spend more time loafing around Greek islands and participating in orgies without clearing up the mess than actually writing anything. However, as a lifestyle choice I was made quickly aware of its limitations, and I don't just mean the occasional drowning (Percy Shelly RIP). So, I began working in IT recruitment instead, which involved a surprising amount of loafing, but not enough orgies.

There are few things more motivational than an open plan office. Forget sunsets, hilltops and breaking waves; anodyne corporate environments are the true muse. Employees beavering away at desks are really people writing novels, rewriting the small print of an office milk whip, or re-juggling their Fantasy Football teams. It was a fertile environment for the imagination, and one in which I learnt the crucial skill of writing while actually doing something else entirely. Rather foolishly in terms of future book sales I eschewed writing about Irish dysfunctional families and their secrets, to write the sort of book I wanted to read – escapist, light-hearted and occasionally, albeit accidentally, funny: PG Wodehouse but with semi-automatic weapons. However, there is huge risk in announcing that you're writing a humorous book in case it's, well, not funny. You can barely get away with a thriller lacking thrills, but a funny book that isn't funny is just strings of sentences.

Like the sun, my novel was something best seen from the corner of my eye. Staring at it directly risked being blinded. Starting a novel before you've written a short story gives you no idea how long it's going to take, nor how hard it is. However, when people enquire what you're doing, it does create an allure of intelligence, so long as it's not your boss, who might have more pressing questions than the hair colour of the protagonist, such as effective use of company time, why you've not hit your targets and why you're practicing your autograph with the flourish of a silver screen wannabe.

Anyway, I digress. I left IT recruitment to follow a sixteen-year career as a mental health social worker. People ask if my novel is influenced by this, and the answer is no. It would be unfair on my clients, and myself. After all, voyeurism in made-up characters is acceptable, somehow less so in real people. I also write for the same reasons that I read: to escape, as walking the streets of Brixton hoping to find disturbed people that you are responsible for is best kept private. After all, meeting a Social Worker approved under the 1983 Mental Health Act to (possibly) compulsorily detain you in hospital under Section generally means the wheels to your life have come off, and who wants to read about that? Not me.

So, I was attracted to the idea of a novel that fantastical, and which did not deliver anything too unbelievable too quickly; so that you are already sucked into the narrative by the time anything unrealistic happened, by which point it was too late. The problem was that being attracted to it meant having to write it. I was careful to place events in a real world of fast food and pop music, so the fantasy never gets entirely out of hand. A Life Assistance Agency has always appealed: a company that does not need to define itself by any specific services, or indeed any viable business plan. The main protagonist Ben Ferguson-Cripps was exactly the sort of customer the Agency dreams of, and this is how he first hears of it in Chapter 1:

I looked again at The Life Assistance Agency business card and marveled at the optimism of a business plan that involved punters not mocking such speculative services. I recognised the card's Impact font. The KLF used it on their record sleeves. Your problems, our assistance Where telephone banking and dietary supplements fail, The Life Assistance Agency succeeds. Private investigation, sick day excuses, situation manipulation, people: lost and found, Life advice, coincidences arranged, hits arranged, soul mates found (special rates apply), final Will and testament

50

re-writing, fear of death minimalisation, account massaging, swimming lessons, Feng Shui and Bonsai trimming.

This is the start of what has been described as a romp, a farcical road trip and the Blues brothers pursuing the Holy Grail, and not just by me, but by readers kind enough to not only find excellent similes, but to put them on social media. The Life Assistance Agency's first case is a missing university lecturer, before the agency in turn discover themselves pursued by a Psychic Society intent on preventing ordinary folk from straying into the occult and messing things up.

It is important when writing to be ambitious whilst remaining realistic – which is exactly the sort of advice that the Life Assistance Agency's proprietor, Scott Wildblood, has spent a lifetime ignoring. And I guess I did too.

Infuriatingly, writing is something you can only learn by writing. And nothing tells you that you're not yet ready to be published like showing it to someone who tells you exactly what they think of it. You ask them to be brutal, claiming you're thick skinned, which proves to be categorically not the case when they follow your directions to the letter and critique your prose like it's a revenge fantasy. It's these bruising moments that sort the wheat from the chaff, which is exactly the sort of overused metaphor that an honest reader will suggest you rewrite. And that always hurts. What doesn't kill you makes you a better writer; you will learn to sleep with the bruises.

How to research ...

Writing a novel is hard enough without needing to know which side of the bed a 15th century London Ferryman slept on. Following don't write from the POV of a cat, the best writing advice is don't write historical fiction, which is presumably why I ignored it, along with all other good advice over the years, like never trust a man wearing slip-on shoes, and don't write books.

I kept historical parts of the Life Assistance Agency to a minimum – four sections of a medieval diary – but it still presented the perfect opportunity to avoid any writing by doing extensive research, eighty percent of which was surplus to requirements. I chose not to use period dialogue either, where everyone speaks with an e on the ende of everything, nor did I chase authenticity by writing with a quill. My characters did however quaff ale, so it was important to experience this accurately.

Another warning. Establishing historical characters is the easy part. Problems arise when they want to discover things. Unlike contemporary protagonists, who can cut your word count by 5000 words via them doing a Google search in chapter three, historical characters have to actually meet people to ask, and spend half their screen time reading heavy tomes under the watchful eye of a moody monk. And that's after learning to bloody read first, which does not necessarily make for scintillating fiction.

Nothing tells you that you've finished a novel involving a historical figure such as Dr Dee like an exhaustive exhibition on him; of the sort I had prayed for when starting my research. It was like finding everything you've Googled in the flesh, well, perhaps not everything. In light of my recent searches for a used car, a garden composter and cheap flights to anywhere, and the other stuff, this is definitely for the best.

Of course, the most frustrating thing is discovering that your fascinating 16th century alchemist and angel-caller isn't your historical figure, but other people's as well. As I said, a memo must have gone out a few years ago, because Damon Albarn wrote on opera on Dr Dee, Peter Ackroyd a book, and Random House eventually declined my novel because they had already signed a trilogy of novels involving, yup, you guessed it: Dr Dee. I got to the party late, but at least I got there, even the revelers had lost interest in anything beyond getting a cab home.

My delayed visit to the Dr. Dee exhibition at London's Royal College of Physicians a few years ago was the stuff legends are made of; if legends were compiled of illness, train cancellations and chicken-pocked childcare. However, facing another day of an ill child and children's TV spent wondering how Noddy secured his pilot licence, and how he afforded a helicopter, while looking for a very specific Lego figure last seen under a rug two years ago, I wrapped up my then two-year old amidst promises of 'going on a choo choo train 'and actually left the house.

On arrival at London's Royal College, the two-year old was chuffed with his lanyard like only someone unacquainted with the need to wear one every day can be. He frowned as I purred at the exhibition's glass cabinets containing what appeared to be neatly labelled 400-year-old recycling. It was actually the reunification of Dr. Dee's library, the largest collection of 1500s England. Dee returned from Europe in 1586 to find it ransacked, as you do if you've chosen the wrong house sitter. Seeing it collated together again was thrilling, albeit combined with disbelief that so many items, only a trained eye would value, had survived.

The exhibition was the sort of thing that confirms how old you are. My teenage self would be aghast at attending. I was stung by museums early doors. A visit to the London Toy Museum is a familiar rite of passage for school children, only instead of having the latest Star Wars figures or the sort of Lego sets available only to the company's executive board, it was filled with items that required a lot of imagination to identify them as playthings. The sort of imagination that ran in the pipes of Victorian England but has since seeped out into the ground water. The Toy museum sees a lot of excited faces arrive and disappointed ones leave. It is a tragic sight; the sort of phenomenon that a good novel captures.

Anyway, like Dr. Dee's stuff, I hope my belongings might be collated one day, preferably tomorrow, as I have mislaid enough stuff over the years to fill at least three medieval libraries. Mind you, if it was collected then it might provoke little more than: 'what's this pile of crap? 'or 'how many broken hole punches is it necessary to own?' And 'why does anyone need 3 copies of Raze's seminal *Break 4 Love* on 12"?' I can actually answer that one, but only on request.

It's hard to know what my two-year-old liked the most. It was either *De lateribus et angels triangulorum* by Nicholas Copernicus, which was protected beneath heavy linen to protect it from sunlight, or the foot-operated pedal bin in the disabled toilets.

The two-year old grew bored before I was able to properly purr at the *actual* crystal ball Dr. Dee and Edward Kelley once used to scry angels; he opted to play with the lift button instead. Yes, a button was more interesting than a crystal ball which had revealed angels to those committed enough to seeing them. Although I guess an elevator button shares a similarly lofty aspiration. There was also a Quentin Blake illustration of Dee from 2011, which easily justified taking the toddler, that and later throwing sandwiches at pigeons in Regent's Park.

However, there was something truly magical about seeing the items I have grown so familiar with while writing *The Life Assistance Agency* over the past few years.

How NOT to write a novel.

1. Wait for inspiration.

This is to be filed alongside 'waiting for the one'. It does not exist. Tellingly you're more likely to meet inspiration than your carefully constructed fantasy partner. The one that you've based on a lifelong stew of your first primary school teacher mixed with the best friend of the love interest in a movie you saw at sixteen. It can happen, for a paragraph to plummet from the sky so complete that it's hard to take responsibility for it, but unless you're Mohammed, it's best to forget all about the mountain and just keep climbing. Like a good tennis return, if inspiration happens you need to be in the right place at the right time, but you can't just stand there in perpetual readiness. All you can do is to ensure you're always within reach of a pen.

2. Plotting.

While it's thrilling to write without having any idea of where you're going, like some idealised country walk in which you follow your nose to discover abandoned Oast houses, badger sets and rusting farm machinery before a quaint pub requiring at least four pints to leave, ambling does have pitfalls. Like the country walk, you're likely to find after a couple of hours that you've walked into a dead end and can't find your way back to the car before realising you have lost your keys and it starts raining.

I never plot and you can tell, or at least my dermatologist can. It's now written all over my face; frown lines deep enough to grow seed in. A good plot is the map that tells you where you are when you get lost, and you will inevitably get lost. However, if you're a writer that only knows what happens once you've finished then you have had the better ride; it will just take longer to comb your hair back down.

55

An unplanned novel is like having Sudoku or a crossword following you around prodding you, demanding attention. It's like an internal video game in which your unlimited lives do not necessarily lead to greater mastery of the game.

3. Look over your shoulder.

Unless you're a fighter pilot it's best to ignore what's behind you. The wonderful thing about writing is what emerges from the forgotten places of your past. And it will happen. Writing taps into a reflective space it's otherwise difficult to contact. The unconscious spills out, with all its neatly packaged metaphors and string puppets. As to literature, the past is littered with great writers, unfinished manuscripts and ash-filled hearths. Light your own fire. See what happens.

4. Ignore the craft.

Solar Bones by Mike McCormack is a book that breaks the rules. It's novel in a single sentence, which presumably only free divers are able to read without taking breath. It's supposed to be excellent. However, if you want to be published it's advisable to respect the rules and techniques of writing, so at least so you know you're breaking them. Story always wins. As does breathing space and punctuation.

5. Take Rejections Personally

Writing is such a fast track to rejections that it feels masochistic. Honest friends and family will tell you first attempts at prose are good, but you can tell they've glazed over and silently praying that you never ask them to read your stuff ever again. And they aren't even obliged to pay for it.

Like anything, it takes time to get good, so don't send your manuscript out too soon. Or at least accept that the best way to realise you have misspelt colossal in the title is to send it out to forty literary agents.

6. Give up the Day Job.

It's hard to know when to announce/admit you are a writer, but it's best to keep it in the Hobbies and Interests of your CV until it's at least in the shops. Even then most published writers are barely earning enough to pay the milkman and are hiding behind curtains until he rattles away flicking V-signs at the front door. The number of authors making an actual living is so shocking that I can't recall the figures. It's called denial.

Even once you have written the book you need to promote it, and writers aren't't good at selling, it is why they are writers. You don't ask window glazers to do origami, but these rules don't apply in the literary world. Once you've stitched together eight parallel narratives you need to then tell the world how bloody great it is and any minute without it in their hands is a minute lost, while wondering how the hell you're going to follow it up. It struck me when meeting John Niven and DBC Pierre how a ease they were with holding a beer and not writing. Outlaws they might be, but there is evidently discipline beneath the artful dishevelment.

7. Naming Yourself.

Use initials if you think it magnifies literary gravitas but hoping you might be googled by idiots unable to spell JK Rowling by naming yourself JK Rollwing is inadvisable – they're probably illiterate. Names are important, but be careful, Kirkcudbrightshire is an excellent name for a solicitor, but less good for a novelist.

8. Stop Writing

The hardest thing to accept is that the first novel you write – yes, the one that cost four years, a marriage and a short spell on antidepressants – is only for you. It's unlikely to ever be published. Like sailing it serves to learn the craft. They advise shutting your finished novel in a drawer for two months so you can then read it objectively. The first one should probably stay there. Forever.

9. Don't change anything.

Like traffic lights that remain long after the road works have finished, there's still plenty to pack away after you've written The End. Even if you like it, there's now the balancing act between ripping the soul out of it at the demand of an agent or publisher to achieve publication and maintaining your artistic integrity (or something). Throwing a hissy fit at editorial suggestions with the charm of paying a £100 bill in five pence coins will not make you any friends.

10. Don't expect to get Published.

This is the tough one. Unless you're serving a life sentence in a high security prison then everyone writes with an eye on publication. However, with the current appetite for misery memoirs, you might be more likely to be published with anecdotal gym visits, or diarising staring at the wall without punctuation. Not that I'm encouraging serious criminality to achieve publication, but we all need a USP.

'All novels should be bleach boned.' Some thoughts on Beautiful Creatures by Lawrence Osbourne.

As a writer I know good reviews hold the same value as a sturdy pair of shoes to a hiker, so it would be disingenuous not to drop in a review of a novel so good that it compelled me to review it, despite my envy at how perfectly this book is executed. Even Lee Childs likes it. Its prose is enough to make me weep into the first draft of anything. Lawrence Osbourne is even likable, despite having written his first novel back in 1987 on an olive farm in Tuscany. In *Tuscany* for Chrissakes. What's not to dislike, and yet he's almost the perfect writer. He certainly has the perfect lifestyle.

Despite being widely unknown, and criminally ignored by the literary awards cartel back in London, Lawrence Osbourne lives the life every writer hopes for. He has seemingly lived everywhere, often while writing a novel with a stray dog at his feet. He has stared at life and said, 'yes' never 'later'. He has however recently stepped into Raymond Chandler's shoes to write a new Philip Marlowe thriller. Let's not forget the wonderful words of Chandler, who never got rich writing, who said writers 'have to fight the impulse to live up to someone else's idea of what they are.'

As for Osbourne, living in Bangkok would adequately answer 'so what attracts you to this job?" but it's just one location he's mingled with. He is the archetypal rakish novelist abroad. Do you want to party at millionaire Riad parties in Morocco? Read *the Forgiven*. If you want a missing young schoolteacher in Cambodia - read *Hunters in the Dark*. I could go on, but in the interest of maintaining a desire to keep living in my own shoes I shall stop there.

His *Beautiful Creatures* is more of the same, i.e., well-poised prose. The eloquently tight observations, often of outsiders in alien environments remain, only this time there's also a breath-taking pursuit through Italy, and (slight spoiler alert) just when

59

you want a gun to feature – an Italian Benelli Montefeltro Silver semi-automatic shotgun no less – it arrives.

We find ourselves with two twenty-something girls elegantly tanned and partly bored on the Greek island of Hydra, who meet a young Arab man who has been dropped off by boat from who knows where. The allure of the unknown, flirting with the rash idealism of youth, soon knits unexpected twists of fate, yet always with an extraordinary lack of judging or self-serving political correctness on the part of Osbourne. It's startlingly contemporary.

The novel hits where many aim, but frequently miss. In place of postcolonial guilt, shades of regretted love affairs and stubbed-out Gauloises, he gives literary fiction a story. And the story is only predictable due to peering into every corner you want it to, as opposed to many novels these days that spend too much time looking in the glove compartment to see the road. There's magnificent sense of place, and anyone who's spent a fortnight on a Greek island will recognise the smell of countless donkey generations, ouzo and the dry scrape of cafe plastic chairs in dockside cafes beneath that ancient Aegean sun.

Lawrence reports that 'novels should be bleach boned', which is exactly the sort of advice budding writers don't want to hear, as it intimates lots of hard work. He then rubs salt into the wound by adding 'it's a question of cumulative observation and lived suffering. It takes time.' Damn him, but at least he follows his own advice. If I'm honest his brilliant and much heralded (by me) last book *Hunters in the Dark* is forgettable compared to *Beautiful Creatures*. He's finding his stride in his late 50s. *Beautiful Creatures* is an absorbing, beautiful and exciting read. Prepare to get lost. And inspired. Or beaten. Some books are so good you can forgive them.

How Important is Blogging?

'It is named the 'Web' for good reason.' - David Foster Wallace

I had little idea what blogging involved when I began. And now I truly have no idea. It started as a promotional tool and resulted in a form of medieval bloodletting. It drains you of surplus words that are otherwise homeless, which is helpful, but is ultimately a distraction from where a novelist should be putting them. Reflecting upon how annoying the bleeping washing machine is might be fascinating at the time, but how about next week? It is useful to establish whether you are a bulletin writer, or an author of books. They are not the same thing.

Blogs exist mainly so you can get annoyed about things and then declare to yourself that you're going to bloody well blog about it, because there's clearly a readership out there for rants on drivers' inability to park without taking up two bays, the impersonal ability of self-service supermarket tills, and who invented mayonnaise. You do need to strike quick. Unless you blog about it within two minutes then even you won't care about how slowly other people walk. You'll have forgotten all about it and the world will tick along none the wiser. Blogs are the modern equivalent of writing letters to the Times.

It's like all those notes in your phone that were Pullitzer prize winning novels at the time, but now read more like a free-associating dead head in 1960s San Francisco mumbling to himself somewhere in the Mission district, whilst waiting for the bus beneath a sky lightening with dawn long after the party has ended.

The spirit of my Idle blogs was to grab the baton from Jerome K Jerome and his 1886 collection of essays *Idle Thoughts of an Idle Fellow*, which predates blogging by at least 100 years, yet pre-empted it. And when I say grab the baton, it was more a case of digging where he had buried it, or at least thought he had, and has since been inexplicable moved. It's always someone else's fault. Apart from a crappy blog. Still, his brilliant title has lived on. And I have nicked it with all due respect for this book.

Did I really blog about eating yoghurt in public? Who wrote those brilliant pieces on an observed life that have seemingly disappeared? I saw which blogs worked better than others: topical ones, film reviews and ones on writing. Although sadly there is only so much writing advice you can give before people start asking why you're not practising it or writing a book on it. Please ignore this last sentence – you can never have enough advice on writing, at least until you've finished this book.

It's tempting to stop blogging, but as any blogger knows, you always return to the viewing statistics like a gambler to the racing pages. Blogging is wandering around an antique market in the hope of seeing something that talks to you, although not literally, unless it's a speaking clock. You bash out opinion in the hope of meeting yourself on the way back. It even works sometimes, but it doesn't necessarily mean anyone else will be interested.

When I still read *the Guardian*, before it became too shrill, I loved the weekly pictures of writers' desks. They would frequently be positioned to provide a good view out of the window. But what can't be pictured is what really happens during writing, and that is what Nabokov described as a throb, which might light the path to years of literary frustration, yet is the glimmer which keeps the project under sail; even if the wind drops, you can still feel the spark. It is discreetly flamboyant. It is the path moving beneath your feet when you are stationary. For a writer the throb is ever-present.

I have blogged about how London is too hot in summer and too hot in winter. I've reported how much I enjoyed a jumper and jacket for the first ten paces out of the house, before needing to carry them both for the rest of the day. I have observed how life is basically spent carrying things, and the definition of being wealthy is not having to carry anything beyond an air of mild expectancy. The capacity of London's tube trains is halved in winter as people leave home bundled up in Sumo cultural appropriation, before stripping it off on the Northern line. There should be lockers at tube stations to ditch coats in, based upon the Amsterdam system of sharing bikes, you take your worst coat never expecting to see it again.

I once went clubbing and everyone kept handing me their drinks so they could dance. I kept telling myself this was not to prevent me from dancing myself, or perhaps they were threatened by my skills. I ended up wandering around like a waiter having lost a table's order. Writing is the same. You carry this flotsam around, and blogging is a good place to store it. You can even rob parts to put in later novels, no one is watching that closely; not even yourself.

Facebook or Twitter?

Writers, particularly it seems those ones inviting *Guardian* photographers into their work areas, are often spotted sitting alongside with a nice whiteboard of post-its of characters, themes, and a framework for their plot. It's intended to make everyone else feel bad. It's the sort of thing that is a good idea for other people. Bloggers don't have them. Are bloggers proper writers? Who knows, but writing anything means you're a writer. And the great thing is that even if you're *not* writing you are still a writer. It is your identity, like someone who runs is a runner, even when they are sitting down. Keep it up, apart from the post-it notes of course. They are nauseating for anyone uncertain of where the current sentence is going, much less the plot.

So, an opportunity to address Twitter, which is a combination of Sunday Hyde Park corner speakers, *Hello* magazine, and a piñata rammed with contention to thrash at with the furious abandonment of people having lost all touch with consequences.

I have been on Twitter since 2007 like everyone else. I joined without really knowing what it was. In my rashness, I may have missed the small print that will eventually claim my corpse for vaudeville, but I joined because everyone else had; just like Panini stickers and opening building society accounts in the hope that I might one day receive shares, resulting in my savings now languishing in accounts that even the building societies are unaware of.

When Twitter isn't a place where character assassination and daily skin flailing are embraced like lost relatives it is where people shamelessly write *'A problem is only an opportunity that hasn't presented itself yet'*, in serious font like Baskerville, when it should be in nothing above Courier. Soft focus photos of unicorns, or burbling mountainside brooks, generally illustrate these platitudes. Any self-respecting unicorn would be pursuing the use of its image via legal avenues with the sort of ferocity that no self-help books or positive affirmation can help with; with the level of aggression no one associates with unicorns frankly. A recent one was: *Don't rush anything. When the time is right, it'll happen,* which is exactly the last thing your employer wants to hear in lieu of a reasonable excuse for arriving to work at lunchtime. It's also an appalling method for baking meringues.

Twitter for writers is the north face to climb. Its population is people furious at their toes being trodden on by life and self-published writers, whom have been encouraged by well-intentioned family members to string never-ending adjectives together in self-published, unedited, unreadable novels about dragon-slaying and maiden-laying knights that they post links to alongside 5-star reviews written by themselves. I understand that we all occasionally need to poke out the rain collected in the tent awning, but sometimes it's better to allow the weight of water to tear the whole bloody lot down and start again.

I wonder why I started tweeting. Initially, the advantage of not actually knowing the people ignoring my witty tweets gave Twitter the edge over Facebook, but it gets to you. It's like saving your best lines for a party where the music's too loud. I've banked on the need to have an online presence despite not knowing what to do with it.

Social media enables us to contact every person alive, yet instead of asking what the Green Party is going to do about Qatar requiring air conditioning to host the World Cup and destroying the ozone layer in the process, we are gawping at camel toes and discussing the virtues of liquid soap while punning #ediblebands.

Then comes the day when you can't think of an interesting tweet. The shock arrives with the sort of misplaced guilt more commonly associated with not having a supermarket loyalty card when asked by the cashier. It's not even as if anyone is clamouring for your next tweet; you're competing with yourself, which is taking 'know your enemy' to new and frankly worrying levels.

65

Collecting followers, (who needs friends), is briefly nourishing, but like a collection of Toby jugs, beyond washing out dust and dead spiders, what do you actually do with them? That's not to say I've not contacted great people, and even made some genuine friends online, but most users seem to be baseball moms, entrepreneurs whom I'm unsure have ever encountered an actual office, and authors who have taken their books' cover design into their own hands.

But the biggest issue with Twitter is that it deludes you into thinking you've had social contact. It affirms your presence, yet you can spend the day without opening your mouth (eating doesn't count). You want affirmation? Pretend this is in Courier: *Turn on the garden sprinkler and you'll find your rainbow.* It might be advisable to find inspiration elsewhere.

Be inspired by the best - HG Wells, and why life is too short for plastic coat hangers.

For last year's words belong to last year's language. And next year's words await another voice. - T. S. Elliot.

So, as the night slipped from one year's clothing into its fresh contemporary cut, the new year's midnight switched from one stream to another. New Year's Eve is never pretty. It is loaded. And no one enjoys a loaded night. My writing had nosedived into mediocracy; I was distinguishing myself from the masses with all the distinction of a grey-finned penguin in a colony of two million black-finned brethren. I was going to use waddle as the collective noun for penguins, but no one would believe me it's true. Google it. I can guarantee this is a better start to the year than reaching London's fireworks early enough to claim a good spot only to find yourself unable to get a drink or take a piss for eight hours.

All New Years are an opportunity to make almightily bold public promises to yourself that you'll fail to live up to. Things like learning how to basket weave, shutting down your laptop as opposed to minimising windows, or to write a novel. We spend too much time in our lives determining to change the crappy plastic coat hangers for inexpensive, more substantial, wooden ones, yet never get around to it.

My second novel *Unfinished Business* was published in 2019, and despite the hype of the first, has not spooked Lee Child or Thomas Harris in the way I had hoped. That said, while they still have a shoulder to look over it's worth persisting, so, it was time to write another. That's not the easiest thing to do when you know people are not reading the last novel; the one that was going to pay for the pool cleaner of the pool that the first novel hadn't afforded you. So, a new year, a new novel, a new audience.

There's nothing quite so motivating than spending New Year in Sandgate on the Kent coast overlooking the English Channel when the neighbouring house is one that H.G. Wells lived in. This is a man who wrote 50 novels and an equal number of non-fiction books. This is a man who has done more than enough to justify a blue plaque on any house he spent more than five minutes in, as that was apparently long enough for him to smash out another 20,000 words. In fact, there should be a trail of blue plaques marking everywhere he walked, crapped and slept before he finally succumbed to liver failure in 1946.

The amount of time he must have spent alone is astonishing, although perhaps writing 50 novels in a 79-year lifetime is testament to the distracting impact of social media on the contemporary writer. At least that's what I'm claiming. I can't imagine Wells had off-days, and if he had writer's block then it's best not considering how many more books he may have written. Sometimes you write dangling on the strings of the literary gods, at others you hit the page with the grace of an egg hitting a bowl. Wells was clearly dancing on more inspirational strings than most.

Having said that, I can see how he may have written so many books whilst staring at the English Channel - I know the French have tried to give it their own name, but no one knows what it is, as it's the blankest stretch of water this side of a gravel-pit puddle. For what is purported to be the busiest shipping lane in the world, the Channel is utterly devoid of life. During my stay in Sandgate a helicopter drilled past towards Folkestone at such low altitude that it might have been possible to untie the pilot's shoelaces. So many people on the beach waved that I suspect its fly-past made the front page of the local *Herald*. It was so exciting that people hung around in the hope they might see its return journey. H G. Wells probably wouldn't have looked up from his page. He had no distractions, not even TV, nor the necessity to move his car every two hours to avoid a parking ticket: true story.

Wells didn't even only write. As a diabetic, in his spare time (!), Wells co-founded the charity The Diabetic Association in

1934, which has since been rebranded as Diabetes UK, presumably because the former was a too complicated name for most people to understand. I'm also led to believe that managed a few affairs. Perhaps he had his own time machine.

Anyway, why not grab every new year by the whiskers. Make those changes, even the small ones, they all count, and most importantly don't settle for less; life is too short for plastic coat hangers.

How to blog successfully

I once harboured intentions to be a newspaper columnist, until I realised that for good copy you need interesting things to happen to you. Not just once, but all the time. Local parks are populated by drinkers, people without gardens, and columnists hoping a dog will run off with their blank notes, or something. Anything really. It's already hard enough spending life waiting for something interesting to happen, but not getting paid when it doesn't is masochistic. It's whole new levels of self-flagellation.

As with comedians, bloggers scan every minutia of their every thought to be rated for possible anecdote, until you realise that drinking apple juice from what appears to be a recycled beer bottle (artisan probably) is the most interesting thing you've done for six months. That's even before you've logged into your blog from a 2nd email address, in order to bolster visitors that only you know the viewing figures for, in the sort of horrifyingly dark spiral that would even have Arthur Schopenhauer spluttering into his nihilism.

It's the occupational hazard of writers that sitting at tables quietly self-congratulating yourself for not having a 'proper' job isn't riveting copy. In the cafes there might be fleeting eye contact with another writer, followed by shared disappointment that it's not enough to fill two words, much less 500. A little later they're probably considering the same thing: whether it's worth tweeting about how uncomfortably warm ears get in decent headphones (tagged under #firstworldproblems). What many writers have forgotten is that they wanted to write because they enjoyed reading, but you don't get paid for reading, they thought, so I'll write. Well, you barely get paid for writing either, so with the pay parity why not stick to what you enjoyed in the first place. Pick up a book, read, smile, and get a job; something's bound to happen there.

Perfection. Of Sport and a Past Time: James Salter

I am creating him out of my own inadequacies, you must remember that — James Salter.

They say you can't choose friends. Or is it family? It's all such a blur. And do novels choose you, or do you choose them? We all have books that feel like our own; as though written for us in the manner of poets once scribing for Royalty. I forget how James Salter's *of Sport and a Past Time* novella fell into my hands, but it wasn't through recommendation, it was more serendipitous than that, a prod from the book god; a right turn as opposed to a left, or perhaps it was just the elegant cover. Actually, it was probably the publishing imprint.

Before being taken over by Random House, the Harvill Panther imprint was beautifully eye catching; black spines, with ornately coloured strips providing it with the continuity of a record label. They provided understatement in an age when covers were designed with the taste of Premier League Footballers' mansions with unlimited funds and over availability of marble.

From their small office in Victoria SW1, Harvill strove to establish a list of classic 20th Century titles fallen out of print or the public eye; a typically idiosyncratic trip with an eye to art as opposed to, unfortunately, profit. Few books came greater than James Salter's 1967 *Of Sports and a Past Time*. Never has anyone transferred their skills from piloting F-86 'Hunter' class jet fighters in the Korean war, to such nuanced descriptions of innate tragedy of human hearts and condition. If they have then they've kept very quiet about it. War teaches you how to wait patiently rather than kill people. And perhaps the fact that days, or even weeks, of pre-operation planning for the sake of a 10 second burst from wing-mounted 12.7mm canons, fed into the accuracy of Salter's writing. It certainly reads like it. It has been bleach boned as Lawrence Osbourne advised us. We can all learn from that. Baden-Powell had it right: be prepared.

71

That the rush of new publications eclipsed this novella demonstrates how older works can become neglected, though not weakened; like powerful slack water at high tide, lost amongst the glory of the break. Another example of this is John Williams' *Stoner*, a novel still sunning itself in the glory of having now sold over 200,000 in the UK alone, without (yet) having been made into a film starring Tom Hanks. That it sold less than 2,000 copies on its publication in 1965 is simultaneously sad and hopeful, yet is an outlier as opposed to the rule. No writer ever secured a loan on future sales.

Of Sport and a Past Time contains my favourite sentences ever written, during which the world pauses breathing, the only noise being birds dropping from the sky; stunned by the beatific prose. It begins 'I have a coffee in the Café St. Louis. 'Which is obviously a fantastic opening line to an unwritten number one record. It later continues:

'It's as quiet as a Doctor's office. The tables have chairs still upturned on them. Beyond the thin curtains, a splitting cold. Perhaps it will snow. I glance at the sky. Heavy as wet rags. France is herself only in the winter, her naked self, without manners. In the fine weather, all the world can love her. Still it's depressing. One feels like a fugitive from half a dozen lives.'

Once I regain breath (it never ceases to pinch), I notice Microsoft spell check has suggested 'consider revising 'some of those lines, which makes me want to shove a hardback copy of Henry Fowler's the King's English into the nether regions of Bill Gates' empire, with protruding steel bookmarks.

With such simplicity of prose and clipped poetic turn, Salter can, as someone once suggested, break your heart in a single sentence, and they didn't mean 'Your girlfriend's left you…for me.' Instead, through netting those fleeting, wordless bewilderments that accompany our existence, James Salter returns them to us processed and flawlessly captured. In the romantic tradition of universal truths uncovered by individuals, Salter captures the hopeless awe in which men are caught when in the proximity of beautiful women, along with the far reaching, and often blinding, strains of lusting hearts.

Most importantly, he celebrates those transient connections between people, those moments when the distances between us are closed. As Michael Chabon pinpointed (admittedly about something else), 'bright sparks might leap across the gap, as between electric poles. And we must be grateful for their momentary light.' This novella is a gentle precious whisper of quieter moments in our loud, overpopulated times. It is the sound of dust setting in off-season hotels and the silence of the ballroom that once swung with life. It reverberates with those memories that make us alive.

Finishing the writing of a novel.

'A story has no beginning or end: arbitrarily one chooses that moment of experience from which to look back or from which to look ahead.' Graham Greene,

Finishing the writing of a novel is the sort of thing that sinks doom into the heart of every writer, whilst hopefully not their readers. Having a novel to write means that when waking up so late that even seizing tomorrow with the carefully rehearsed baseball catch pitched by a presidential candidate seems distinctly unlikely, you still have purpose.

Finishing a novel, unless you're being paid to, makes as much sense as cocaine in the shower; it might feel clever, but it's just a soggy, expensive mess. And what happens next? It all seemed a good idea at the time.

There's nothing better than having something needing to be done and not doing it. It's the inspiration of Jerome K Jerome's *Idle Thoughts of an Idle Fellow*, who inspired these thoughts. Completing a novel means a snatched moment of internal celebration, a sort of awkwardly misjudged hi-five that thankfully no one is privy to, before the hollow realisation that you have, well, nothing to do. Obviously, you send it out to as many agents/publishers who are foolish enough to find themselves googled by you, before noticing that the only consistency in the manuscript is erratic spellings of 'intrepid 'and recall them all.

You resend to what might as well be Spam@publishinghouse.com. As with having a healthy hedge, or a healthy hedge fund, there is a huge difference between writing a novel and writing a publishable one. Once completed, you are confronted with the reality that perhaps it is inadvisable to inform your boss to go fuck themselves and leaving their employment for casting the Hollywood adaptation.

74

Writing a book is the mental shed that you can disappear into to potter about and discover what's really going on in your head, and even write that steamy sex scene that'll never make the final edit, of either the book or indeed your actual life. With a novel on the go, you're a novelist wherever you go, but once you finish? Well, you're just another dreamer doing nothing about it. It's just you and a blank page, accompanied by the sense that the first book was fluke. Not that it was finished. You don't complete a novel, you abandon it. You drop it from the balcony hoping it'll fly.

It's amazing how after six years and twenty FINAL edits that work remains to be done. Generally, over the course of its existence, the pages will have been written drunk and edited sober and written sober and edited drunk. It will have needed a new ending requiring a new beginning (and middle), a lead character gender change, a six-month writing course, the comments of twelve friends (one of whom you are no longer speaking to), three relationships, two children and two cars, yet it might still be considered a fluke, but such is the human psyche.

Unlike the French essayist Jean-Jacques Plachet, who was so desperate to finish his book that he shot himself in the foot with a hunting rifle to stop himself from wandering away from the desk, I have no scars, nor a limp to regret. While the internet beckoned irresistibly with its sultry long fingers, once you have nothing to do *but* indulge the allure of Hedgehogs in Hats, or Hot Girls Go Hiking, it soon pales. Writing becomes an attractive distraction.

A novel on the go is a comfort blanket that validates all kinds of things, some of which aren't staring into space. You can sit in cafes to pretend you're on the Paris Left Bank, instead of London's South Circular. You can people watch, and answer dinner party enquiries about your vocation with a vague/detailed reply that you're a novelist, depending on how closely the enquirer works in the publishing industry (or might know someone).

I remember a neighbour who used to own a Range Rover. When I say Range Rover, it was a metal lump rotting on the front driveway. It was more protruding geological strata than a car. It was impossible to get into his house without squeezing past its rusting hulk. I'm unsure he even noticed anymore, but he could still claim to own a Range Rover. Writing is the same. While you're working on a novel, you can claim to be a novelist. Once it's finished, it becomes someone else's, another more industrious version of you, which you ponder and admire whilst searching for similar purpose. And there's nothing worse than doing nothing because you have nothing to do, and I'm unsure reading publishers 'rejection slips counts.

How long does it take to Write a novel?

The short answer is bloody ages. This might sound obvious, but just as it is sometimes necessary to poke a pencil in your eye to confirm it hurts, occasionally it is required to write a novel to establish how hard it is. The unwritten Life Assistance Agency loitered in my life with the entitlement of teenagers at a bus stop. It was long enough to be transferred from at least two computer hard drives and irreparably jam up an office printer.

For many writers, looking too closely at how long it takes to complete a book is inadvisable without emergency services on speed dial. One of the popular questions people have for writers is 'are you writing another one?', which makes you wonder why you started all this nonsense in the first place. Despite your wildest fantasies, there is no sea of adoring fans at Red Rocks under a blood crimson sky, or name drops from major interviewees in primetime TV interviews clamouring for another book. There's simply people idly wondering if you're going to write another, as though it's on par with having another sausage roll at a party.

I recently read a fascinating interview with Will Menmuir – a Booker Prize long list nominee – who wrote a diary about his writing of his book *The Many*. It is an honest account of how a first draft barely makes sense even to the writer and the daily 500 words goal (as per Graham Greene) he was lucky to meet in a fortnight. I have no idea how honest it is. His novel seems to have lots of ideas but an unwillingness to pursue them. Perhaps that already captures the novelist's milieu. In light of the time spent writing a novel it's almost unseemly how quickly you forget the arduous process. Balancing prose, characters and plot is akin to traversing a room whilst avoiding the floor. It's basically sticking with an idea that you fear might be shit with no one yet to tell you otherwise.

I always intended my Life Assistance Agency to be a series of books from the instant that the Commissioning Editor at

Random House asked me if it had sequels. It was one of the most exciting meetings of my life and involved a free Kit Kat. The Random House offices in Vauxhall Bridge road even had a canteen. It was so old school that I half expected Don Draper to wander in drunk. The Editor was so interested in the novel that he had asked me to meet me. If I'd had other plans they would have been dropped like a hot coal. We sat down and he explained how interested they were in signing franchises. My heart juddered with the realisation that my novel was a standalone. But, not for long.

I made up the sequel's title *Blind Fury* on the spot, which led to the idea of having a retired wrestler Billy 'Blind 'Fury as a character. See what I mean about having potentially sketchy idea and sticking with it. He appeared so perked up by this that I added a third book to the rapidly growing trilogy. Thankfully he did not enquire further as I'm still working out how to complete the trilogy ten years later.

Since Blind Fury was the working title, I also toyed with title ideas such as *the Life Assistance Agency and the Loneliness of a Pop Star*. It echoed Herge's Tintin books – *the life Assistance Agency in Tibet*, etc, which basically looks like a thinly disguised excuse to go travelling for 'research'. I've been long obsessed with what successful pop stars do once their moment in the sun inevitably fades and they're left with the mansion, a swimming pool modelled on the shape of their own ego, and unsold signed copies of their final album occupying the sauna.

Since the publication of the first novel, I was aware of needing to write a follow up. I had already completed 40,000 words of *Blind Fury*, but decided I needed to start again from scratch. I'd like a word with the version of myself making that particular decision.

The hardest thing to find in writing is your voice. It eventually arrives, but only after more false starts than the Millennium Falcon. I always wanted to write novels as thin as the cigarettes

I was smoking. Some kind of treatise on the human condition that hit home truths like Steve Smith smashed runs in 2019's Ashes. Instead, I now aim to write wry, entertaining adventure yarns of the old days involving angels, rusty revolvers and cravat-wearing villains. The most annoying thing about this is that I don't read novels about angels, although I do think *Stigmata* is an amazing film.

To be honest the angels are coincidental. The novel is really about a pair of chancers setting up an agency in the same spirit that pioneers once set up record companies, publishing houses and dentists. Hang up a sign and pray people will come. Like Douglas Adams wrote *Hitch Hikers Guide to Galaxy* in the Sci Fi genre, the angels are really simply a vehicle for some adventure, jokes and absurd predicaments.

I hope this book captures some of the sporadic nature of the creative process: the self-doubt, sweat and tea stains of writing a novel that might be called the Late-Night Loneliness of a Pop Star. It's hard to know when I thought it might all be a good idea, but writing a good line always helps. It can be simply be a line that throws a life ring into the thrashing water. In this case it was:

'The yellow Daihatsu was hurtling up the driveway as though driven by someone looking for dropped sweets in its foot-well. '

I only had another 30,000 left to go.

How to use music in your novel

I'm not afraid of being thought of as someone who is associated with film music. Why not? If it's a good song, what does it matter. - Bryan Adams

You might wonder what relevance music has to novels, but it is so often through books and music that people identify themselves; to define to refine who they are. The bands and books are the badges and football colours; often for those who don't play football, but not always. They signify your tribe and even your pace. They capture a time that people are reluctant to let go of; a moment in their lives when identity was achieved through a band tee shirt and a well-rehearsed carefully placed literary quote. We are what we eat, and are what we have heard and read.

There are clearly more important things in life than musical taste. Just ask Gavin Rossdale after he joined the Voice; presumably at the cost of being able to sleep at night ever again. Yet playlists remain central to our lives. When I say 'our 'I mean people that consider compiling mixtapes as integral to their lives. Those that consider it as an important weapon in their courting armoury. After all, if you can't say it yourself, then let a 30-piece orchestra, pounding drum machines and a bass line louder than war to do the talking for you. These are people that even in moments of crisis will be thinking 'I wonder which song would best soundtrack this?' For these people Billy Idol's *Rebel Yell* says more about them than their CV ever will. Those songs of our youth are set as though scrawled in cement.

A novel is no different. It needs songs. Of course, most writers, and car salesmen, are failed musicians. I should know, I've been both. Not that I was in a band for long. Gothic Poodle was a mistake from the name down. None of us could play instruments, yet that did not stop us from amassing a back catalogue to rival no one's. We split up over creative similarities, although *Runaway Girl* remains an unrecorded classic, at least in my head. She had the sun in her air is all I can recall, which I assume was not the tabloid set loose on the wind. I still want to start a band called Shouting at the Radio, but I can't sing or play, or even shout for long these days without needing a throat lozenge. In my first book the lead character found himself in a band, the Mournful Horns, but was never involved in the songwriting, or even band naming process. It has no bearing whatsoever on the story, but these details are useful for the writer to know how the character might respond later to a conversation about ruptured dreams, or if an evil dictator demands that he play a piano.

One has to be honest about influences. That can take time. No one wants to admit to preferring the Rutles to the Beatles, or Bruno Mars to Drake, but everyone comes clean eventually. It took me a long time to accept that my influences are not Bergman or Camus, the Left Bank or Bob Dylan, but 2000AD comics, Smash Hits and *Highlander*. This 1986 film is best known for being the only watchable film Christopher Lambert ever starred in. It features a sleek soundtrack from Queen including *A Kind of Magic* and the statuesque *Who wants to Live Forever?* It is this song that cued up my first novel. The practical issues of eternal life underpin the premise of both my published novels. Who wants to live forever? is a question anyone pursuing immortality is unlikely to have fully explored.

The challenge of asking Queen and Freddie Mercury to write music for my books was mitigated by the fact they had already done so in the shape of *Highlander*. Freddie has also passed on, in one of rock music's greatest losses, so I'll never know if he'd have agreed; I'd like to think he would have. However, their soundtrack made a great starting point. My protagonists are keen music lovers, so Bruce Springsteen rubs shoulders with the apt Oasis' *Live Forever* and Robbie Williams schmaltzy *Angels*, which not only healed a Britpop rift, but anchored the story in real life by playing Radio 2 in the background.

The novel found itself with a soundtrack that could have written the story itself, that's if playlists were able to write novels, which sadly they are not. But they do help. They provide the story with rhythm, even if it is with songs you don't like. Just don't spend too much time choosing songs for unwritten scenes, just write the damn thing.

I took things one step further with *Unfinished Business* featuring its retired pop star. After all, who hasn't wondered what happens after your huge hit single and all you have on your hands is time, and money with which to fill it. After all, there are only so many Rolls Royces you can crash into a swimming pool before it starts to impact your fitness regime. You can always buy a quilted Chanel water bottle at £5,000, but you only ever need one, and even that's at a push. Wealth doesn't enable you to make a more expensive cup of tea, it remains tea and it certainly cannot buy more time, and it certainly doesn't excuse you from death, heartache or indigestion. Money does not make a tea cosy any cosier.

It was on completion of the novel that someone suggested I compile a soundtrack. Annoyed I had not thought of this myself, I noted every song as it appeared in the book, and did so, while adding a few extras. I wish I could claim this did not take up an entire day, but like writing a novel, it needed to find its own poise.

Now, talking of making a cup of tea.

How not to make a cup of tea.

Under certain circumstances there are few hours in life more agreeable than the hour dedicated to the ceremony known as afternoon tea. 'Opening sentence to Henry James (1881) The Portrait of a Lady.

I've rattled on about declining standards in tea-making for longer than it takes to brew a decent pot. People I've harangued about it certainly thought so. After all, if it's important enough for George Orwell to write evergreen advice on how to make a drinkable cup of tea while brutally addressing communism, aspidistras and paeans to his perfect pub the Moon on the Water, then teamaking is a clearly an important subject.

When I was a social worker tea drinking was very much part of the job or at least I thought it might be. I wouldn't say it was what attracted me to the profession, but it was certainly up there with doing some good in the world. Two main skills I developed during this time was to ensure I never stepped away from my pen in an open plan office, and to always politely decline tea made by someone suffering from a relapse in their psychotic illness. You could always tell the evergreen newbies to the profession. They were the ones politely accepting a cup of tea from someone attempting to present as calm after extracting imaginary cameras from the wall of their flat using a masonry drill and hammer. Accepting it might actually wise, but the drinking of it less so. I sometimes wondered if it was a patients' method of measuring a professional's experience in the game - it was the ones subtly not drinking the tea who know what they're doing.

So, the rules of tea:

1) The only person who can make a decent cup of tea is you. NEVER get anyone else to make it. This can be tricky, as tea is the first thing most people offer you on arrival in their homes, that's if you've been invited in and they're not calling the police.

Upon invited arrival, deny you want tea, before waiting ten minutes, then politely suggest you'll make one yourself. If your hosts insist on making it, ensure you stand near the sink, so you can surreptitiously pour it away.

2) How to pour away the tea someone has made you carries its own subtle criteria. Ensure the sink has no cloth in it, or you'll be explaining to your host why their dishcloth is later spreading milky, undrinkable tea all over their work surface. The preferable way to dispose of tea is at the same pace as you would drink it. Despite your sense of self-importance, not to mention that of the tea, after ten minutes your host will have forgotten all about it, so it can disappear unseen. However, this has not yet addressed the issue of making a good cup of tea.

3) It is crucial to stress that the best avoidance of other people's tea is via meeting them in the pub. I would suggest the Moon on the Water, had it not been appropriated by a chain, with the sort of identikit chalk boards that would leave Orwell sleepless. Anyway, in pubs no one thinks they can do better than beer brewers, apart from the lonely home brewers, so it's a level playing field. However, this is not always possible.

4) So, as ever, even with tea making, timing is everything. There is such a thing as teatime. Despite coffee taking over the world it has not yet been given a specified time to drink it. There's no coffee time, which perhaps explains people drinking it from dawn to dusk, manically wishing they knew when they should stop. Teatime is so idiot proof that insipid tea making is inexcusable. Teatime falls at about 3:20pm with an hour window following that. However, despite there being an actual teatime...

5) the best time to drink tea is probably first thing in the morning. When I say, 'first thing', I mean the first thing you do upon waking, not at 00:01. Sometimes, if your teamaking is up to scratch, you might seep poorly in anticipation of your morning cuppa.

Of course, (see point one) generous people occasionally like to make you tea, even at 7am, so it's tricky. It is advisable to either have a bedroom with a sink or print off these rules and 'accidentally' leave them out.

6) Equipment – Fresh water, tea bag or leaves – let's not be purist about this, there are more important battles, such as the china. It HAS to be bone china. I'm risking snobbery here but if coffee drinkers can publicly ask for a latte-mild-chocco-hot-bot-half-shot without pronouncing the hyphens, then this bone china rule has to hold. Although-

7) china cups are not necessarily needed. Not only do they fail to hold enough tea, but the exact angle of your superfluous little finger informs those in the know exactly which college you attended at Oxbridge. Or not.

8) A thin bone china mug is perfect, so why use anything else, unless you're offering tea to builders – no offence, but I doubt they hand out their best china to people handling wet cement for a living either. They get the heavy souvenir mugs better suited for surviving when dropped from scaffolding. Builders generally have a better insight into where you've been on holiday over the past ten years than your best friends.

9) The next crucial thing is to leave the tea bag in. Presumably there's some directive demanding that coffee shop chains wave tea bags above the water with all the intent of a water bird declining to land. They then slosh in enough milk to douse a housefire. So, tip 9 is really – LET IT BREW. You want it strong enough to require teeth bleaching to remove the stains.

10) Add only a SMALL AMOUNT OF MILK. A SMALL AMOUNT OF MILK cannot be stressed enough, as I've just demonstrated by using needless caps lock. Sugar is optional, but only if you're trying to prove a point, and keep your teaspoon employed. Best is half a level teaspoon of brown sugar, which offsets the bitterness to the tea enough to maintain it.

11) Of course, this brings up the subject of the teapot. The teapot is increasingly used in TV dramas as an indicator that it is a period drama. Either that, or as a prefabricated home for mice on CBeebies. However, it remains a staple for anyone serious about their teatime, but for some reason seems out of place and overambitious for the morning cuppa. The best contents of an afternoon teapot are three parts Assam, one-part Earl grey, and definitely not anthropomorphized field mice wearing their Sunday best while sliding down the spout.

12) To truly appreciate tea, it's best to limit intake. It's better to spend time anticipating a cup of tea, as opposed to never letting a cup go. Ideally – drink twice a day. When you need it to wake up, and to counter the mid-afternoon slump at teatime. It's why it is placed at that time of day. Drinking tea twice a day means that while you're not drinking a cup, you're anticipating it, which for anyone who survived the Star Wars prequels, will know is a far preferable state of existence.

Oh, and to stress the fresh water. It's been rubbished in the past as being pedantic, mainly by me, but now I'm sold. It makes a far superior cup of tea.

Things people always say to writers

Someone recently commented that I look like a writer, which I tried to pretend wasn't shorthand for appearing socially inept, malnourished and skint. They studied me with interest and asked me what genre my novel was in. The 'what genre is it? 'is a tricky one to answer, as it's something you realise is important far too late and posthumously try to squeeze your novel into. With little idea how to categorise my novel I considered Adventure, Humour or Chick Lit (is this still allowed?). It was based upon little else than what I liked than what might sell. Although I spent my teenage years reading novels, these would now be labelled YA. I'm unsure I'd have enjoyed them so much had I known how cynically they were aimed at me. Apparently, there are such genres as cat fiction, which isn't novels written by actual cats, but probably even worse.

The enquirer still studying me then asked if my novel had taken me long to write. I thought that I'd answered this previously, but did not have my notes with me. It is what people always ask when they discover you're a writer. There's only one way to answer this and that's breezily, as though you're commenting on an amusingly shaped cloud in the sky. It's important not to look haunted as you reflect upon how long it did take you and then actually tell them. Make it look easy. Enjoy the fact they are interested in you being a writer. It's easy to forget what a glorious moment this is. Just as a cricketer fails to notice the grain of the bat like they were once mesmerised by, you might have been a writer for so long that you forget what initially seduced you. You may have been a writer for ten years, but for the person you've just told it's been ten seconds. Bask in the magic of that.

There is no denying that writing a novel, or at least claiming to, is impressive to people. It remains rather quaint that a pastime which peaked fifty years ago still holds some sway, as though a novel continues to survive as an encapsulant of all that is good about the world. I can see a metallic future that still winks a subtle curtsy to the boundless literary word.

In fact, there are so many regular questions that people invariably ask upon hearing that you are a writer that it might be advisable to have well-prepared answers, which makes my lack of them even more inexplicable.

The most common question is: 'are you published?' as though it's something that inevitably happens to every writer. You want to grab them by the lapels and scream 'do you have any fucking idea how hard it is to get published you imbecile?' It's not something you choose as an option at A-level. Generally speaking, if a writer is published then you don't need to ask because, in case you missed the blanket promotional bombing across every social media platform available, then the airborne banner advertising and their T-shirt emblazoned with I'M PUBLISHED! they won't have.

Once you've caught your breath, and the questioner looks less like they have stuck their head in a Rolls Royce RB210 jet engine taking off, they sometimes add that they've had an idea for a novel too. This suggests that given the opportunity they might bash out a draft too, but they're too busy with more important things, but it's there, on the back burner. At this point it is advisable to keep schtum and not throw yourself across the table to strangle them.

Are you published? is the most dreaded question, and probably the one driving most writers in their pursuit of publication, so, they can answer, yes, I am actually as though it is an option chosen at A-level. It's the fuel in the tank. Publication validates writing and justifies your claim of being a writer; an admission that is otherwise whispered through cracked fingers like you're admitting to having chopped up a body before leaving it on a Dartmoor roadside.

Another favourite is 'How do you find time, with kids, job, etc, etc? 'This is a slightly judgemental intimation of 'are you still doing that?' dressed up as a good-natured question. It also sounds like 'are you looking after the children adequately?' I wish I'd noted this subtlety as a social worker enquiring after children, whilst surreptitiously pouring their tea down the sink. It is also impossible to answer without sounding conceited, (yes-aren't-I-amazing that I manage to juggle everything-including-kids-and-writing. Although not literally). Although it's said with good intentions, you wish the earth would swallow you up. You start mumbling something about the fact they could do it too if they tried, before realising that you sound like a total wanker. The worst thing about being a writer is that most people think you are clever, or a wanker, whereas in actuality it takes you two months to draft a sentence you are happy with, which ironically is exactly the sort of thing a Wall Street grade wanker would say.

As any writer knows, the real question is 'what would you do if you were not writing?' Mind you, never declare this in earshot of your live-in partner, who will produce a list of things you could be otherwise doing with the sort of haste more associated with preventing a child from running into traffic.

What's it about? is also commonly asked, like they are deliberately attempting to publicly shame you into realising that despite having written 80,000 words, this remains a question you have inadequately investigated. This realisation occurs half-way through explaining what it is about, and you need to fake a coughing fit to avoid looking any more stupid. That's if they haven't wandered off already. Agents love a strong elevator pitch, but for the first four years of writing my novel there was no skyscraper on earth with a lift high enough to describe it; not even in Dubai. The best way for them to find out what it's about is to read the sodding thing.

Another favourite assumption is that you are wealthy. This often occurs when you're at the bar, although writers are generally only at the bar to have a drink bought for them in return for a detailed reply to being asked how they got published. No writers make money. Some do, but they aren't the tip of the iceberg but the tip of the penguin's beak atop of a 200,000-tonne ice behemoth.

After a few years of writing, you realise how important it is to tell no one. Not even yourself Just scribble; let the words fall from your mind like parachutists from a plane. They may not all land together, but they'll end up happily and invigorated in the pub at some point. Just trust that. Or get shot down by barrage of anti-aircraft fire.

Why Writers Should Never Attend Job Interviews

The drawback with work is that it happens when you could be doing better things. Never say this at a job interview.

It is important to interrogate yourself as to why you wish to be a writer; about what is driving you into such a strange and invisible pastime. It's no career path unless you are extraordinarily lucky. If you are blessed with good fortune then perhaps it's advisable to play it, at least until your luck runs out, but no one starts writing to make a fortune. People can smell it a mile off. Writing is the whetstone and a knife that takes years to sharpen. It is also the knife's handle; the wood softened by experience of a sweaty and assertive grip.

You might be your own boss, which sounds like a good thing, but unless you work for the Local Authority's Parks Dept, do you really want a boss who allows you start gardening simply because the sun comes out? Because stopping to smell the bloody roses doesn't pay the mortgage. And nor does writing.

I recently applied for a job, you know, it was a quiet day on social media and sadly the Life Assistance Agency doesn't really exist; although if it did it would probably be attempting to hook its car keys from a drain with a coat-hanger. I wasn't entirely sold on the job application process after it took 30 mins for the agency to find me in their own reception. If they can't find me at the appointed time in their own building, then what chance did they have in finding me a job?

I was busy stuffing my face with Foxes glacier mints generously presented in a bowl when a woman called Megan asked if I was Tom, before realising she had forgotten my surname. To her credit she pressed on:

'Are you Tom.. someone?'
I paused. 'I'm Tom, but who has Someone as a surname?'

Megan had no answer to this and the ride up in the lift was, well, let's call that tense. I was tempted to pitch my novel, and it seemed a similarly inadvisable time to inform her that people have called themselves Mr. Amazing by deed poll, even King Arthur Uther Pendragon, although the less said about StopFortnumAndMasonFoieGrasCruelty.com the better. Yes, she exists, and presumably owns a credit card longer than her arm.

Megan disappeared to photocopy my original documents as proof of my ID before I could claim, along with voters required to provide ID, that it infringed my civil liberties. She left me to complete a questionnaire which included the question: Can you give an example of a time when you have done something you weren't proud of. I shit you not. They actually asked this.

Well, I could think of several occasions, some quite recent. I was still sucking a glacier mint and my pockets were rattling with them. Perhaps the mints were a play, some kind of test. I stared at the question like it was a joke. I half-expected a Harry Hill voice over. A social care recruitment agency was asking me the sort of question I struggled to ask myself. Did they mean that time I nicked my Dad's car while he nipped into the pub? Or worse? I mean how was answering this question honestly going to assist me in *any* way to secure a job? I was pleased not to be a Catholic and wondered if anyone had ever answered it truthfully. I scribbled some nonsense about the time I had been not proud of under-claiming overtime in a previous job and handed it over.

And that's the thing with being a writer. You can answer questions that you'd not dare otherwise. Your characters might be unsavoury, flawed and irritable so you don't have to be. But the best advice ever given was do not give up the day job. Do not neglect the other parts of your life in name of finding your creative flight path. If you are serious then get a job that enables the writing. If the number of memoirs leaving the main chamber are a measure, then an ideal job for a writer would be an MP. The House of Commons too frequently looks emptier than a pub nearest the football ground two minutes after kick off, providing ideal opportunity to write. Although, being your own boss means you don't get free Foxes glacier mints, and there's something to be said for that.

The importance of a good title

I thought writing a novel was hard. Try naming it.

We know the difficulty in naming things, and I don't just mean first thing in the morning. It has been speculated that the first spoken words by humans were mother, bark and spit, although it's unlikely they were in English, and how researchers concluded this is hard to know. Echoes in ancient caves perhaps? Without labels we are lost in a world of objects. Since Ug first turned to Ug and pointed at Ug, it became clear that it was important to differentiate some things from others.

Naming is what humans do, it is a defining feature of our dominance of the planet, we go around naming things and then often kill them. But that's not to say it's easy, naming I mean, not driving species to extinction. The Americans often get it wrong, what's with eggplant as opposed to aubergine? While Eskimos found themselves with too many words and too few things to name, so chose to distinguish fifty types of snow, which is still about thousand less words than the English have for rain.

Car manufacturers commonly struggle with names. That there was a meeting at Renault in which the *Twingo* was agreed as capturing the essence of a new model is the sort of brainstorm that those participating in have since drowned in vats of the finest Burgundy. At least they retain the ability to look people in the eye, unlike those involved with the Ford *Ka* naming development programme.

Meanwhile, HP clearly don't struggle with product names, such as the snappily named dv8000z printer, but then I guess you don't spend pub conversions recommending printers to friends; that's reserved for books, films and bands. The arts all live or die by their name; it doesn't matter how good the prose is. If a book is called *Mr Front's Behind* then no one will be reading it.

There's still a list of unused children's names in my phone, which makes naming future dogs easy, although they all answer adequately to 'Oi.' Dogs I mean, not children, they tend not to answer to anything beyond the age of five. However, book titles are far more important than pet names. Titles need to be catchy, intriguing, and not been used before, which is a shame because George Orwell nabbed them all. Of course, no one ever judges a book by its cover, (which is why illustration remains a multi-million-pound industry), but the title needs to promise everything even if it fails to then deliver on it; a pretty cover is easier to forgive than a clumsy one.

Annoyingly I have titles for several books, which means I may have to write them, or at least give them to other people to write, in the hope they don't do a better job and put me out of work permanently. For the duration not having written a word my version will be always superior. You'd be excused for thinking this may have helped when looking to name my second novel, which ended up with more names than Eskimo snow. Of course, asking people for opinion only confused things, as they all like different ones, and never my favourite. A Twitter poll of alternatives doesn't help, you just get loads of support for the title you put in as a joke to provide some balance.

Pet Shop Boys 'Neil Tennant frequently names songs after books, *Can you Forgive Her?* for example, but that doesn't help when entitling other books unless you want to test 'there's no such thing as bad publicity via a copywrite infringement court case.' Perhaps songs are a good inspiration, but then there is also the Ronseal approach when you blatantly state your intentions, but if my new novel did what it says on the tin, the tin would read – *The Life Assistance Agency abandon their USP by refusing to scry for angels, opting instead to write biographies for fading pop stars, yet become entangled with 400-year-old unfinished business*- which is definitely too long as a title.

And there it was. The title. It just tumbled out like a child's dirty washing after a camping trip. Unfinished Business. It's always good to write, even if it's a blog post or a shopping list; you never know what might emerge.

How I got published.

Every writer has a different story to tell, but their favourite tale is always the one involving how they got published. Their least favourite is the arrival of the first royalties cheque, but that's yet another story.

I've been published for long enough for the novelty to have worn off, (actually this isn't true, I'd bite the hand off anyone offering me another publishing contract), but I'll never forget the email. As a therapist I cannot help but ponder that the pursuit of a publisher is the pursuit of an available and encouraging parent; one that holds you in mind at all times and returns your calls. However, it grew rapidly apparent that the publishing house I signed with was not one of these idealised parents, but one who had fallen drunkenly behind the sofa. What a buzz those first few weeks were, when I discovered that dreams could come true; albeit dreams that take ten years to write and edit. I was even able to finally read those articles on' How I Got Published' without wanting to whack the magazine against the table until it disintegrated. The journey to publication are inspiring and galling in equal measure and here is mine.

Over the years I managed to gain and lose two literary agents. I felt as though I was made of titanium when I signed with a literary agency, at least until I lost my shine and they slowly lost interest; distracted by other authors with a clearer idea as to what genre they were writing in. To misquote Oscar Wilde,' To lose one agent may be regarded as a misfortune; to lose both looked like carelessness. They were keen enough for me to sign a contract with the intention of claiming 14% of my earnings. It seemed a lot, but perhaps it should have been three times that to encourage them to be more involved. Beyond handing me their business card I can't remember anything else they did.

Any creative pursuit is riddled with risk. 'Never give up' they cry, perseverance will win out. But it doesn't. Not always. If it did there would be millions of Harrison Ford's (who was a

97

carpenter in Francis Coppola's office where George Lucas was auditioning for Star Wars). For all those that succeed there are tenfold that do not make it. For such a prevalent experience it is startling how the frequent 'failure' is swept under the carpet. The success story is the fairy tale; it is the one we all believe and even encourage one another to believe. But, there is no shame in giving up. In fact, the real skill is in knowing when to give up. How much happiness is there to be found in hapless pursuits. If you can be happy in creativity itself, in the scent, then keep your nose polished. But do not allow it to spoil those achievable pursuits in life.

A few years ago, an actor friend told me how he was giving up his pursuit of acting, and I was struck by what a momentously adult moment this was; to surrender those aspirations of his younger self. Well, I reached a similar moment. Over two years I had sent *the Life Assistance Agency* to enough agents that I had reached Z in the literary agent lists and stopped making any notes of where I had sent it. Any advice of submitting to only four or five agents at a time had long-since been ignored. My mailout had the accuracy of a ticker tape cannon at a 4th July parade.

Through an acquaintance Random House showed an interest, which they probably regretted as I consequently followed them home every night. However, the meeting involving the free cup of tea and already-mentioned Kit Kat in the Random House cafeteria, which was the most exciting thing to have happened during my writing endeavours. I have certainly never eaten such an exciting Kit Kat since. It was only beaten by a cake with the cover of my book on it to launch the WHSmith Fresh Talent that it was awarded in 2017.

Sadly, this was the peak of my involvement with Random. They had already recently signed a novel involving the Elizabethan alchemist and magician Dr. John Dee, and there was fear of overkill. They also wisely declined to provide me with this writer's home address, which might have risked another kind of overkill.

At this point I put the manuscript to pasture, and started another novel, set in a small tenement block in London Bridge, called *the Age of Entitlement*. It was at this point that I asked myself where I was finding the time. It featured a social worker who goes insane. It was a good idea until I realised it was an unfocused diatribe against the unimaginable sense of entitlement embedded in the public sector and its utter lack of imagination and vision as to how it might best help its service users. It wasn't a pretty read, and not just because it took place in the neglected meeting rooms of town halls and hospitals ripe for regeneration. The scaffold on which the story was hung was too obvious.

Actually, getting published feels like the glowing perfection of a film's first act, before the second act is declared by a Boeing 747 crashing landing onto the family house. This is how it happened for me, getting published I mean, not a passenger plane crash. It was so cliched it's hard to write down, but to delay that let's consider the creative chase.

Once I had finished the social worker novel I glanced again at *the Life Assistance Agency*. It was at this point that any observer would groan at magnitude of cliché. Yes, I decided to give it one more chance. Just as I was about to throw in the towel, I intended to give it another edit and tidy up, before sending it to every agent/publisher in the country foolish enough to publicise their address in a sort of mailshot more associated with general elections.

There were no takers, but during this time I was building up a Twitter following, mainly by making friends with people in the hope they might return the interest. Once I had gained 2000 followers a newly found friend suggested Urbane Publishing as a publisher happy to consider manuscripts without agent representation. And it was while buying tickets to see *Hotel Transylvania 2* with my son that I received the email I thought I would never get. My novel had been accepted for publication. I celebrated by buying the four-year old an ice cream he never thought he would get, and won't have again, unless film rights are requested.

And it so happened. The first thing I did on returning home was to hoick the *Writers 'and Artists 'Yearbook* into the recycling bin with a satisfying clunk. And spent the next nine months endeavouring to not fantasise about selling enough paperbacks to cover my expenses and to avoid calculating my hourly rate.

It felt surreal; all those dreams and aspirations now to be made public; not to mention my prose. Annoyingly, the moral of the story is to never give up. I'd become a platitude. Your dreams can come true if you work hard enough. My Victorian forebearers would have been so very proud. I was about to discover what budding writers pursue and what it's like to be published.

What it feels like getting published.

In light of writers often appearing harangued by missed plot opportunities and other even more unspeakable pains, it's interesting how I have not met many pessimists writing literature; it doesn't quite work. Optimism is not optional, but essential, like agility in an ice skater. Sure, writers soon look browbeaten by the deficit between their aspirations and the reality of their success, but they go into it thinking they'll be great. If you don't look too closely at the numbers, you can ignore that only a handful of writers account for selling majority of the books. Mind you, aspiring writers still think they will be the ones who sell millions. Sure, they will. There's nothing like assuming the warmth of the room while peering in from the cold outside. Every fisherman assumes their catch and every collector thinks they will complete their Panini football sticker book by the close of the season. Hope springs eternal.

All good things come to those who wait. I had thought this only applied to those queuing for a massage. If you're intending to wait until you're published, then you may as well write a novel while you're waiting. There's a lot of loitering involved in writing; you have to sit still but let your mind fly. There are so many spinning plates it's hard to keep track.

No vocational advisor has ever recommended anyone to become a writer. As a career option it sucks like a Dyson factory, but as a pastime there is nothing like it. So, when you send out the polished manuscript to agents and the rejection emails are crashing in quicker than a Twitter pile on, you abandon that endearing hope. Then it happens. The sort of good news you've been waiting so long for, yet not long enough to have properly rehearsed a suitable response beyond a sort of gasp.

Astonishingly, my manuscript got two positive responses from different publishers. They were fighting over me, not in some cutthroat auction, or aggressive all-expenses paid lunches, but via pleasant emails. One was a vanity publisher that required my financial investment to help them promote my book. It was unclear what they might bring to the party beyond a beady eye on my profits. Ha-ha. With hindsight it's even harder to know what they might have been interested in. Perhaps they were involved in their own dreams of reclining whilst stroking authors' own cash as promotional activities. Having politely refused their offer of ripping me off I received another email from an independent publisher, who had apparently read the book AND liked it. This was a combination that my self-image and constructs of the world following years of rejection had not encountered before. Some research quickly revealed them to be a) not completely insane, b) enthusiastic enough not to require me to bankroll my own promotion, and most importantly, c) were genuinely interested in my novel without me holding them in a headlock.

After re-reading their email eight times to ensure it wasn't as grammatically incorrect as at least the first four drafts of my novel, I let out a whoop that did little more than demonstrate my lack of practice in whooping. As a social worker I had little opportunity for unrehearsed whoops. It's vaguely alarming to discover that fortune does indeed favour the brave, or at least those willing to rewrite the same story eight times, leave countless drafts on hard drives of NHS computers, and divert tax-payers money from Health to the Arts by running office printers dry.

Bravery and foolishness always dance closely. It's disconcerting, that a book that had been attracting the levels of enthusiasm generally reserved for trying to read a newspaper in the wind, was now liked by someone other than me on a good day, or drunk. It felt like having haphazardly pursued some mythical creature, only to discover it is real. Invariably it's at the point of capturing a unicorn that you wonder why you hadn't thought to bring a horse box to take it home in.

In between staring at the email, I spent the day keeping my mother off the line in case Spielberg's casting agent was trying to get through. I was so delighted that I struggled to suppress a smile. I'd waited so long for this day that the lack of fireworks coursing through the sky was vaguely disconcerting. The world was still turning. Oyster travel cards still sapped my bank account like nets leak wind, and I was still tripping over children (my own I hasten to add) with the sound of cheerios crunching underfoot, as opposed to white sand and crisp Seychelles hotel towel vouchers. There remained only 24 hours in the day, yet only 7 at night, and the postman continued to leave a 'sorry you were out' card during the only five minutes I left the house.

The evening after I met my publisher, I was the out of hours social worker who spent the night in Kingston A&E department trying to persuade a woman onto an ambulance until 6:30am, while all staff, including police and security declined to touch her, despite her being on a sec.2 which allows for reasonable force to be used. 'Don't you know I'm getting published' , I wanted to scream, but the professionals were too busy avoiding work to actually do any. The only person showing any interest in me was the patient, who lay on the ground refusing to get up. I drove home with my head in my hands, if that's possible. I was so tired I still have no idea how I did that.

It is easy to spot writers recently told they are to be published. They already have a knife ready to open the delivery of paperbacks and no longer fear the question: 'So, what do you do?" Where once there was a mumbling: 'I'm writing a novel..', like a guilty secret shared with the wrong person, there is now a puffed-out chest, and the search for opportunities to shoehorn, 'I'm published', into conversations that haven't even started. I was unsure what to do first – get a t-shirt printed with VINDICATED, or I'M PUBLISHED on it.

Then was the issue of when to celebrate. On the initial news? This would have involved popping a bottle of champagne in the cinema full of half-term toddlers trying to decipher the script of *Hotel Transylvania 2*. Or perhaps when I signed the contract, which was at 8am, not the ideal time for a celebratory drink unless it is the final one of the night. Either way, the real celebration was in the moment when I finally held the paperback in Autumn 2016.

My name was on the cover, and my picture on the back. I could not stop looking at it; some strange alchemy had led from some spurious ideas about immortality and a Saab into an actual book with a spine and acknowledgements. Good things do come to those who wait. It just depends upon how much waiting you're willing to do, and what to do while you're waiting. It was too easy to recall Noel Gallagher's words on releasing the debut album by Oasis. 'After Monday, when the album hits the shelves, we're cursed to be eternally bored.' He said, already aware of the double-edged blade of success and the end of dreams.

How to write the acknowledgements

In the on-going spirit of following the writing journey and making it up along that way, much like parenting, I find myself at the acknowledgments. They present the ideal moment to reflect upon how the seemingly impossible task of writing a novel was accomplished and who helped, while avoiding the full bewildered overwhelm of Gwyneth Paltrow at the Oscars. It's also a gold-plated opportunity to really piss people off.

As any writer with more than one published novel will know, the acknowledgments are a minefield that makes the previous 80,000 words look like a stroll up an escalator. It's not exactly learning to play the three suites of Liszt's Années de Pèlerinage on a harmonica, but it feels close. As someone (possibly) once said about maintaining relationships: it's not what you put in, but what you leave out. And boy there is opportunity to leave stuff out of the acknowledgments; it's stadium-sized opportunity to leave people off the guest list.

Established etiquette, not to mention the threat of lawsuits, demands a roll of thanks to the people who have bank-rolled, tolerated, and in one instance carried the writer out of a bar. It's the time to praise all the other names which should be in the front cover alongside your own. And it ensures a renewed motivation for friends and families to read at least two more pages of a manuscript they hoped to never see again.

Because not quite believing your novel will ever get published means the acknowledgments are a hurried, yet important afterthought. You don't want your joy at publication ruined by forgetting to thank your wife/husband/rector.

One of the drawbacks of taking years to write a novel is that there are plenty of people who get forgotten. Some might even be dead. Meanwhile it's opportunity to forget the ex-girlfriends, cab drivers, Scout leaders and that bloke who once foolishly sat next to you on the 44 bus with whom you shared an early draft, leading to his subsequent retreat from human contact and culminating in a drugs and alcohol addiction that continues untreated to this day. I hear the passenger also remains traumatised.

Generally, the last thing a writer wants is names other than their own on the cover. Even the title is a compromise, unless you're Jonathan Franzen, whose novel you might be forgiven for thinking is called Jonathan Franzen as opposed to *Purity*. This is why acknowledgements appear stuffed reluctantly at the end. However, there are few clearer signs of an amateur writer than one who declines to recognise it takes more than one person to write a book.

However, once you start acknowledging it becomes hard to stop, and avoiding the 'Gwyneth' becomes harder. If you find yourself listing future family pets, then this moment has probably been reached. Unlike a successfully established novelist, it is inadvisable to thank your fans in your debut novel. The fans are essentially your parents, and Aunt Linda. So, at this stage it's important to thank supporters by name. I know at least 13 office printers that have been decommissioned as a result of the volume of printing manuscript drafts, but they'll be forgiving of their absence in the thank yous.

The appearance of my 6th form English teacher Mr. Blake took me by surprise. Regrettably he has died, so is ignorant to the subtle influence he had on my literary life, probably correctly thinking I spent too much time looking at girls in class to be appreciating the descriptive low-pressure weather fronts of Jane Austen's novels. We read so many plays - six Shakespeare when only one was required - in his lessons that it grew apparent that the only thing he had never read was the A-level syllabus, but his passion was clear.

Names I've forgotten to thank kept me awake at night, and I was at risk of so many names appearing that I might need to do the acknowledgements for the acknowledgements. Now, where's that harmonica. Actually, in future I'm going to thank no one but me. I took on the trails of an idea and made it smoke. It was all me damn it, and no one gets left out that way; at least no one important. I thank myself.

The problem with terrible novels

Some books are best left forgotten…

Anyone else feel bad for hating a novel? There is a school of thought that suggests you should always finish a book. And when I say school, I mean the internalised monolithic institution that casts a shadow from childhood to old age; the one that pulls your socks up and tightens your shoelaces. It's unclear where this idea of always finishing a book first emerged from. Perhaps it started when families owned only one book and if it was your turn then you damned well made the most of it; with the pages needing to be plied from your hands as you read the acknowledgements for the fifth time. Or perhaps writers made it up; imposing the idea into the minds of children, so that no matter how appalling your novel might be, people will finish it. Not because it's good but through a sense of duty that fears public scorn.

It's hard to remember bad novels because the good ones make such lasting impressions that they thankfully obliterate the memory of the poor ones. The only impact bad novels make are on the sides of recycling bins. The worst thing about them is the attention they're stealing from all the good books.

I'm not going to name many names, after all, I'm a novelist. I know how much goes into writing a book. For many writers real life is just noise in the background; simply material with which to sculpt stories and tricky plot knots. To be told that abandoning family, career and house maintenance to live on a mountain probably wasn't worth it might be life shouting too rudely for comfort. For others of course it's just an opportunity to close the door and cruise the internet, yet still expect 5-star reviews and similar adulation to those writers that ate nothing but bamboo shoots in the name of research.

To be fair it's all a matter of taste. To some people my novels are a glorious collision of the Blues Brothers meets Da-Vinci Code, while others think it's really good. The clearest sign that a book is rubbish is when you're accompanying the reading with sighing sounds. Pages are turned with the sort of dread familiar to anyone who has to take young children swimming later in the day*. I'm pleased no one has yet compared this with mine.

There was a time when I felt obliged, in accordance with that unwritten code inscribed in stone atop Himalayan mountains, to finish any book I picked up. It has certainly made me more cautious in which books I know handle. I've been more loyal to books I dislike than friends I like. This once meant trawling my way through *the 91 principles of Cataloguing* when I mistakenly held it for someone while they jumped off a bridge. To be fair it was a textbook. Mind you, even that's preferable to Morrissey's novel *List of the Lost*, which somehow exceeded his own autobiography in verbosity, making sex sound like the sort of substance found stuffing Victorian cushions. It read as though he had just thought to himself, how hard can a novel be, it's just words. He's correct, but proved they do require joining together.

It's always awkward when friends recommend a book that turns out to be less readable than a doorstop. Handing a book to a friend to read is like the black spot. You may never see them again. You sometimes return a book with a vague nod at having enjoyed it, praying that they don't press you for enlightening thoughts on what happened at any point beyond page 32.

It's hard to be objective; one man's *If on a Winter's night a Traveller* by Italo Calvino is another's *50 shades of Grey*, and to be honest it's hard to slag off books when it's admirable to find people still actually reading rather than scrolling through tik-tok videos of people instantly changing their outfits. However, the idea of reading another novel encompassing cross-generation Irish families with hidden secrets makes me want to actually suggest taking the kids swimming.

Bigger targets are the easiest to hit and the aforementioned Dan Brown's *Da-Vinci Code* really is unreadable to anyone who likes English, sentences and words. One of the best examples of

109

him failing to capture an instantly recognisable human experience is:

'He could taste the familiar tang of museum air – an arid, deionized essence that carried a faint hint of carbon – the product of industrial, coal-filter dehumidifiers that ran around the clock to counteract the corrosive carbon dioxide exhaled by visitors.'

Although, if most people walk into museums, sniff the air and think 'is that the arid, deionized essence carrying a faint hint of carbon? 'or 'how corrosive is my breath exactly? 'then I've been kept in the dark. Or rather in the night-long gloom that envelopes sentient beings with an inability to envision where they might be traversing in the dim blackness, as Dan Brown might put it. The book is so bad that even Ron Howard and Tom Hanks couldn't film a watchable movie of it.

It was at this museum point that I decided I had better things to do than read about Robert Langdon running through corridors and libraries and thought I'd do something else. Like anything. Even DIY or glossing. Or even bloody writing some of my own prose, which I reasoned couldn't be any worse.

However, you have to respect a man who found success only with his fourth novel. Dan Brown stayed in the game, despite once asking if a bookshop wanted him to sign a copy of his 2000 novel *Angels and Demons* to be told no, as they'd not be able to return it to the publishers unsold if it was signed. He found success by putting his head down and keeping his hands busy and researching air conditioning. He writes every day, starting so early that he's done by 11. Sadly, there is no getting away from the fact this is the only way to write a book. One line at a time, plodding into the storm, as the wind blows the snow over your tracks.

Perhaps it is sensible to get in with pre-emptive attacks, like Daniel Pitts' book *The Most Boring Book Ever Written*, which almost demands contrary critics to argue otherwise. It is a title so sure of itself that it demands the book to be read. After all, surely it can't be *that* boring. I'll report back.

The Evening Standard described Hanif Kureshi's *The Last Word* as 'brilliantly funny'. Now, I'm aware that daily reporting of London stabbings might cloud your judgement in relief at those moments when you're not, but it must have been a quiet day in the office for the self-absorbed protagonist, who changes characteristics quicker than you can keep up with them, to be described as brilliant, much less funny. Mind you, Kureshi might think I'm lucky to have my novel alongside his in the few book shops stocking my novel, and he'd probably be right. He's successful while I'm neck-deep in redefining the concept of diminishing success. His books are still stocked by Waterstones, whereas mine are more likely to be found in the bric-a-brac stall in a home counties local flower show.

This is a true story. I was leafing through old paperbacks without any intention to buy them – they were twenty pence each which seems too cheap for anything – when I saw a cover I recognised. It was *the Life Assistance Agency*. I picked it up for long enough to encourage the volunteer to offer a further discount. I took her offer before she was paying me to take away my own book. Mind you, it'd be the most I had made from it since my royalties. I slunk away to tell my mother. It was only then that I realised it had been her copy donated to raise money for a new sandpit in the local recreation ground.

Writing music reviews.

There are times in our lives so glorious that even while they occur we should have been pegging them to our soul in the knowledge that these luminescent periods have a battery life. For me it was free music, not only free, but pre-release promos. No one gets free music forever, not even the most legendary of music reviewers, of which I was little more than the post-note fallen to the carpet and lost its stick. I wrote album reviews for the BBC, and gig reviews for various websites run by highly motived and knowledgeable boys barely out of school. All for love and not money. I never got paid, but it was my favourite job. I remember once booking a room to see a patient at the Community Mental Health Team I worked at to interview Sarah Cracknell from Saint Etienne, on the phone I hasten to add. Insert *He's on the Phone* (their biggest hit) gag here. I did the short interviews for the *Metro*. Fast Talk I think they were called. It was a chance to interview people I thought were famous. The newspaper often disagreed with my analysis on who was worth speaking to.

Having spent most of my student days on the run from accrued Blockbuster video fines, the focus and motivation in these music website boys exposed my own early twenties in an unfavourable light, but I was willing to forgive them if they threw me gig reviews. As they were unpaid it consequently didn't require me to write to a next-morning deadline. This was fortunate as I spent the next day hungover, deciphering my phone notes made drunk in a crowd, while fielding calls from service-users requesting they were released from hospital and demanding food vouchers. Social work and music never danced so close.

I soon found a nose, and thankfully an eye, for writing reviews; after all I'd spent my life reading them, so for once I was prepared. So, I had learned to read between the lines. Tame Impala's 2105 album *Currents* was a unanimous hit with the critics, being described as sparkling with kaleidoscopic experimentalism. It even reached no.3 in the album charts, unless returning my vinyl copy to Rough Trade slid it to no.4. Rather than the joyous sound of someone redefining pop, as had been described, it sounds like someone's fallen asleep on a synth arpeggiator. In a rare display of subtle solidarity not a single reviewer had a bad word to say about it.

Reviewers have mellowed since the 80s/90s reviews of NME and Melody Maker, where hangovers, indigestion or missing a train would result in the sort of damning judgement more suited to high court verdicts of a particularly horrific murder case than the description of a ropey debut album. Mark Beaumont's review of Kid A by Radiohead (considered a classic) was that it was the sound of Thom Yorke ramming his head firmly up his own arse, hearing the rumblings of intestinal wind and deciding to share it with the world.

The classic question to expose pop stars' slim grasp on reality is to ask them the price of a pint of milk. Equally, you might ask music critics the price of an album, although sadly that applies these days to anyone under 30.

I've been reading music reviews for longer than I've been buying music. A limited teenage budget meant it was crucial not to buy a dud. It required reading between the review's lines, and *experimental* is an example of a key word that actually means – run a fucking mile. Experimental means that a band has turned its back on what initially made them popular – MGMT for example – and breaking the golden rule of show business: Give 'em what they want. Unless, of course, they thought fans actually wanted self-indulgent psychedelic guitar noodles akin to driving a tune blindfolded into the desert and forcing it to find its own way home.

Summer is a good time of year to release music, as critics aren't listening in cities at temperatures suited to the throat of volcanoes, but a breezy poolside, which is an environment particularly forgiving of under-par song writing. So, I really should have known better than buy Tame Impala based upon unanimously good feedback. It's the season for the phrase feel good in reviews, which means catchier than Velcro, and the inability to remove it from your head until autumn. It's also a phrase that's impossible to read without thinking of Beach Boys or the Boo Radleys.

The skill to reading music reviews is to look for key phrases. The *difficult* 2nd album means the band have been too busy spending tour bar tabs without realising it's coming from their rapidly decreasing record company advance to actually write any new songs. Meanwhile, the *grower* album means it has no hit singles on it, and the sound in the background is record company execs screaming down telephones to prolific remixers asking if there's any chance of a catchier radio edit.

As a reviewer you need to be careful when writing an *overly enthusiastic* review, which might be the result of writing too near, or even during, a memorable after show party, where the lead singer is briefly your best mate and whom you're telling is the best front man since Freddie Mercury. You wake up in the morning with a hangover that could walk itself to the medicine cabinet and a review that the band will never live up to. Ironically they'd be more likely to remember you if you slagged them off.

Another warning word is the *concept album*. At the time of its release the artist will be convinced their magus opus will change pop music/destabilise governments/redefine capitalism forever, but actually ends up about as interesting as two men on cocaine talking about golf, albeit with overblown cover art and six producers who's only success is no longer being on talking terms with the band.

Often, following this, is the *Return to Form*, which is a band *returning to their roots*. This means belatedly accepting what people want from them, i.e., to sound like themselves and not some other band. Other bands often have that covered. There'll be a rewrite of their biggest hit and instruments are played with fingers crossed that the fans haven't abandoned them. Then there's the *Personal album*, which means a lot to the artist but little to anyone else. It's often the sound of divorce lawyers licking their lips, unanswered answer phone messages set to music, or in the case of Marvin Gaye's pithy *Here my dear*, heart-bled soul with the royalties going to his ex-wife.

Of course, any female artist who writes and produces her own stuff with a touch of the ethereal is instantly compared to Kate Bush. If men were similarly judged, they would be constantly compared to David Bowie. Meanwhile, anything that has a chance of getting played on the radio without causing upset is dismissed as Middle of the Road, despite this actually being a very dangerous place to be.

Christmas is an easier time for everyone, including critics and pubs, as it is 'rinse that back catalogue' time. There's the Greatest Hits album, which sells itself, and the cover versions or duets album that sells the artist short. These albums are so artistically redundant that the record company executives might as well be singing the overplayed cover versions themselves. The covers album seals artistic redundancy; a farewell note written by someone else. Annie Lennox's last album of standards included *Indigo Blue* ('woke up this morning and I'd be better off dead'), which simmered with all the anger of someone who had narrowly missed their Ocado delivery slot.

Another tip to music journalism is to never review genres you know nothing about, particularly jazz. Purists will know if the trumpet's reed is real cane or synthetic, who made it, why the farming family initially embarked on supplying to the wind instrument industry, and why their products never recovered from the river reed shortage of 1967. So unless you also know this, do not say a word. You can never blag a jazz cat.

The sad fact remains that the review is often the best thing about an album, so sit back, and enjoy what you think the music might sound like without ruining it by actually hearing it.

115

The elusive rules of book writing.

Here we are, the overriding theme to the book. It's my experience that there is nothing writers like more than rules. It gives a framework to a pastime that has none. It's the signage where the terrain lacks any. Successful authors simply scribble out some rules that they claim to have followed when asked to do so by a Sunday newspaper and later sling them to hungry wannabees from their gilded balconies. It's ironic really, that writers chase certainty, when their chosen pursuit requires stepping out of the fast lane and, if not into the slow lane, then certainly onto the hard shoulder for a good long cry. At risk of confusing writing with Mad Max, where you're going there are no rules. Deal with it. You make it up as you go along.

Rules suggest that there is a secret formula, a few nods and you're heading in the right direction. We know the only rule is to sit down and stay there until you have written loads, anything else is sugar quantities in the icing on the cake. Rules only really help when you're slumped below your desk hunting for notes that you're not entirely convinced you ever wrote, but definitely should have.

A good guideline would be to know what publishing houses want to see in submitted novels, but as they have no idea themselves until another house has unexpected success with a novel they previously rejected, this will never happen.

A helpful rule to counter this would be that other people provide the entire plot of a novel to write and ask you to crack on with it. Some publishing houses even do this, asking for regular updates on how you're getting on, before informing you that their high concept idea, which had been absolutely perfect for you, was actually better suited for someone else; someone else who hasn't just written 80,000 words and not had emails ignored on a weekly basis asking for *slightly* more revealing feedback than 'maybe look at this bit again.' If it is impossible to understand what an editor, who has asked you to write their own

116

idea, really wants, then what hope is there of knowing what an un-surveyed public want to read before they have?

As I've said, writers love rules, and a good example of them is Ronald Knox's ten commandments. He was a clergyman, so it is easy to trace back his influence on this idea. He was a member of the Detection Club with Agatha Christie, Dorothy Sayers and G. K. Chesterton, so assuming they had not corrected his rules, these guidelines are gold standard, albeit in their reference of a Chinaman, rather dated. You can find the commandments on the internet, but to not use more than one secret room or passage is priceless. Don't make things too hard to believe. Allow there to be consistency. He's basically advising against the idea of ex machina. Never take the easy way out. Writing is the opposite to airline safety procedures; always ignore the nearest exit. If the hero has to make a choice always force them to take the second one.

The other useful commandment connected to this (not by a concealed corridor) is that no accident must ever help the detective, nor must he ever have an unaccountable intuition which proves to be right. Resist this ex machina; everything must have a tail, and not appear as though in answer to a prayer, because it is only answering the author's prayer to be rescued from the dead end. Resist. Never fly because you can't dig yourself out. Let the reader feel as trapped as you do, and who can then sigh with pleasure at the clever ease with which you free the protagonist. What they don't see – the clenched fist and sleepless nights – does not concern them.

Andrew Motion was right when he advised to write for tomorrow, not for today. Reading is delayed gratification, and with writing this is magnified. It's a tough life lesson, and writing serves it well; that sacrificing short term pleasure for long term gain places your feet firmly on the foothold of life.

There are hundreds of rules out there and many say the same thing. This book is another collection of them, but what they all amount to is: know yourself. And it is through writing that you will know yourself, your preoccupations, your desires, your ambition and your discipline. You may not want to know, you may have been drawn to writing to maintain not knowing, but writing exposes it all, and you can't hide from yourself, not forever. You will read back on your books and realise how much of you lies hidden between the lines.

What to do while awaiting Publication.

No one is treated with more patronizing condescension than the unpublished author - Tim Parks.

You've waited all your life to get published, so what happens next? At least attempting to not look smug is most important, although it's hard to write this in fear of sounding conceited. I'm addressing this by not writing WHOOP! every other word. I am doing knee slides, but you can't see them.

Achievement can be as hard as striving for it; ambitions are strangely hard to replace, even with success. The days following the news that my novel was signed were spent telling shopkeepers, bus drivers, even unattended petrol pumps that I was getting published. But, what to do for the next ten months until the paperback is in your hand, and hopefully half a million others? Spoiler: this bit didn't happen. I managed a second print run, but things ground to a halt on that summit. I think I may have sold 4000 books. This is better than none, but it's not a lot.

The greatest question facing a novelist is: does getting published justify wearing tweed? Wandering around wondering if you look author-ish, is, I hope, a promising start. A pipe might be too much, and the egg-stained shirt is already covered, if you'll excuse the pun, but it's surprising how, well, normal writers look. Perhaps these other people in supermarkets are authors too, waiting for the opportunity to confess it with well-practiced self-deprecation to the nearest checkout. Oh, what am I doing for the rest of the day? Probably WRITING my SECOND NOVEL. The only audience for this will be the security guard, welcoming a break from watching the CCTV camera in the foie gras aisle.

I considered hanging my publishing contract around my neck, but I don't want to get egg on it. Perhaps I should have worn a polo neck favoured by intellectuals, although taking them off (polo necks I mean) involves removing a layer of facial skin and utterly ruining your hair. The urbane creatives with their frowns smouldering as effectively as their Gauloise might suggest internal wrestling with existential tension, or which font to use in considering the relationship between Man and his God, but in fact is simply consternation in how they are going to remove their jumper without irreparably wrecking their quiff.

You think everything will change once you're published, but the greatest surprise is that the world keeps spinning. Planes generally remain in the sky; children still say they're hungry moments after having refused to finish their food and there's no San Pellegrino sparkling from the kitchen tap.

I still need to practice my autograph. Yes, it's no longer a signature, which is something I wish I'd had the foresight to see when I practiced signing my name aged thirteen because everyone else was. That it appears to be the last act of an arthritic hand on its death bed did little to encourage a second attempt. My signature might as well spell out: Will This Do. It has steadfastly refused to evolve; an eternal reminder of a moment in time. Flies dying in ink write with more consistency than my signature. Any novels of mine holding any value will be the ones I didn't scrawl over like I'm endeavouring to get the biro to work. Hemingway apparently said, 'write drunk, edit sober', but his advice on book signing is unclear. On heavy sedatives probably, but my scrawl already appears to be written by someone failing to resist unconsciousness.

However, I was positive about its publication, not with the over-optimism of a razor seller in Shoreditch, but having already sold 250 copies on pre-order, I sensed great things were afoot. The lead-in to publication was like the phony war of 1939, well, at least without the imminent invasion of southern England, and the amassing of battle-blooded panzer divisions on the French coast.

Life goes on. Audi drivers still refuse to flash anyone out onto main roads and I'm still missing the doors when trains stop at platforms, but I sensed a tremor of possibility, as though a Porsche engineered kettle counts towards owning an actual Porsche. If I'm honest, I was most looking forward to a buffet with my name on it written in pineapple chunks and melon.

Finding room in a publisher's schedules can be as long as two years, so ten months was a relatively short run-in time, but it remained long enough to forget what the novel was called and why I first wrote it, which was the sort of question I was bound to be asked in the relentless promotion schedule. The lead in is however however the sweet spot between achieving publication and the reality of the sales figures. Sadly, the promotional schedule mainly involved me writing blogs on a vast variety of subjects that always led to the same place of hoping to flog my book.

I'm sure there are several sensible things it is advisable to do while awaiting glowing reviews and world-conquering sales, which don't involve daily googling your own name, but you may not find them here. It would be sensible to start your next novel; a writer writes every day, even if it's simply clearing their throat. And it gives you a head start when the fans devouring the first book are clamouring for more. At least that was how I saw it.

How getting published changes your Life. Or not.

A person who publishes a book willfully appears before the populace with his pants down. If it is a good book nothing can hurt him. If it is a bad book nothing can help him. – Edna St Vincent Millay.

It's hard to not sound conceited when writing about getting published; it throws you into the sort of company that you had previously wanted to stab in the forehead. It is however a postcard from a place you'd be foolish not to write from.

Publication day is the sort of day that validates all those annoying motivational Twitter status updates involving 'following your dreams', and 'Stars can't shine without darkness.' The sort of updates that no one says to your face in fear of being strangled, and without which Twitter would be diminished to people daily declaring themselves as coffee addicts, uploading photos of cats and flogging vampire novels thinly disguised as porn. Or is it the other way around? Oh, and the sort of political bust-ups from which no one emerges from unscathed.

The crucial start to life as a published author (have I mentioned this yet?) was to not spend it on domestic drudgery like fetching milk from the corner shop in my pyjamas whilst resisting the urge to ask 'd'you know who I am?'. The newsagent would have every right to nod and say Yes, I know who you are, and you still owe three months arrears for weekend newspapers. Once I got back from the milk run, I stuck to my plan of leaving London for the day.

I pulled up outside my local book shop where the paperbacks had been delivered. Kindly they had not opened the box, aware that the writer, in a moment of rare practicality, might want to open it themselves. I bloody well did too, although it did feel over-rehearsed as the staff watched me do it. The second indication that I was not yet widely known as a published writer was on a Shell forecourt off the A20.

I had been off social media for almost 50 whole minutes due to driving, so was keen to catch up while fueling the car. I had barely tapped the multiple notifications on Twitter when a Tannoy announcement suggested I stop using my phone by the pump. The fuel supply was then cut off. Pretending I hadn't heard and had actually intended to fill the car with only £4:32 of diesel, I strolled across to pay.

'I turned your pump off because you were texting. 'the cashier gleefully announced.

'I wasn't texting, 'I said more petulantly than is advisable once you're over the age of six.

Anyway, I was convinced she would imminently recognise me as a published author justified in checking Twitter news. But she didn't.

'Why can't you text? 'I asked.

'Because it can cause a spark. 'she answered.

'Has that ever happened? 'I replied, "I mean, a petrol station blowing up from a sparking mobile phone? 'It was restraint unremarked upon that prevented me from adding a mobile phone belonging to a published writer.

She stared at me. 'Look at YouTube. 'she snapped, like I was the only person left alive not having watched a series of petrol stations exploding through someone checking social media at the petrol pump. I fully intended to remedy this once I got home.

It perfectly illustrated how nothing had changed. I reached the beach hut for the day and basked in, not the sun, but validatory social media likes and congratulatory comments. It was a bubble bath of brief admiration. Before I even left to drive back to London the likes began to slowly ebb away, leaving me bereft.

It was only a matter of days before the Texaco public address systems had silenced, to be replaced by the sound of breakfast cereal, bills dropping from the letter box and cracker crumbs crumbling underfoot, as opposed to the Seychelles white sand I had imagined. There were still only 24 hours in the day, most of which I was spending not writing, and I managed to cut my nose shaving, which made it a day of two firsts.

Publication is a fence I had been running to leap over for twenty years without any thought as to which way to land – forward roll, the splits, or career into the nearest gorse bush to emerge from quicker than I went in. Time will tell, but at risk of sounding like one of those positive affirmations, publication day was one to savour.

It was certainly a day to quit worrying about writing. I had done it. It was one of those rare moments looking at the ground while crossing the finishing line and not at the next hurdle. It was a day like no other: *the Life Assistance Agency* was in my hand,

Most writers would claim that is the best day to start writing the next novel. Which is lucky, because the most popular question since publication is 'Have you started a 2nd one? ' Perhaps then I'll be allowed to text at the pump.

The literary festival

The Life Assistance 2017 UK tour had three dates. World domination postponed.

It was hard to know from which angle to approach the invite to my first literary festival. I decided vertically, but barely. I often find the literary tent as the most companionable place at music festivals, it is a reliable place to escape people emerging from being cooked overnight in tents who think dropping class A drugs is a sensible alternative to a cup of tea and croissant. So, to find an entire field dedicated to the written and spoken word was nirvana, particularly as my name was on the bill. That there were no bands to miss while asking authors what side of the mug they drink from was a bonus.

I was to be interviewed by the charming literary commentator Paul Blezard, at the delightful Curious Arts Festival in Hampshire and to say I was nervous was like announcing wasp stings hurt.

I was emboldened to find that my appearance at 1pm in the Arcadia tent was following a whiskey-making class. And it was raining, so finding a pissed up captive audience in my tent couldn't have been better planned. However, they had clearly drifted off to find cigar-making class, or some barley in order to crack on with some fermenting. Nonetheless a welcoming crowd met me, albeit a sober one.

I read out a chapter and got a few laughs that weren't from my companions, before a warm and pleasant conversation with Paul, during which I heard myself publicly admitting that I had deluded myself into thinking I was not writing a humorous novel in case it failed to be funny. Afterwards I even signed some copies and spoke to some glorious people who were so defined because they had read (and thoroughly enjoyed) *the Life Assistance Agency*, and keen for a sequel, which was fortunate as it was already scheduled for publication the following year. I appeared to have already sold one copy.

The highlight was signing in the Waterstones tent. Feeling like Bono must feel on a shopping trip in Dublin, I was walked across to the substantial tent by Paul, where I saw a long queue of people alongside my book. My heart kicked, but it was the second glance that revealed the queue to be for the till, which simply passed my book. The second highlight was someone asking me to sign two copies and saying how much she had enjoyed a particular scene. It's a magical moment to encounter the location where your propelled words landed.

In addition to the promotional opportunity, the organisers were kind enough to provide a spacious glamping tepee, in which we rolled out Snooze 200 sleeping bags amongst 500 copies of the programme with my name on it. Despite the headroom and space, glamping is still camping, and the night was spent restlessly dreaming of the Snooze 400 sleeping bag, while trying to change sides on a camping bed two inches narrower than my body. I have never understood why camping seems to be a good idea. You bring so much equipment that your house is stripped bare, you spend the weekend nailing down temporary inflatable floorboards, annoying neighbouring tents, but otherwise you are permanently too hot, cold, or damp, often inexplicably all at the same time. You can hear other people murmuring in nearby tents, which sounds far more interesting than the murmuring in your own tent concerning where the hell the toothpaste is and why a fox has run off with your shoes left outside the tent.

Having two children with you thankfully prevents you from agreeing to a glitter make-over at 5am in the dance tent, although plenty of parents were happy to make the most of their compromised situation by blocking the exits to the main tent with pushchairs and trolleys of snoozing kids during the music act of Tom Odell, (an alluring mix of Elton John gorging on early piano house). Other parents had spent the day making do with getting pissed in the kids 'tent while their offspring made papier mâché masks and cadged money for face painting. It may not be a good look, but a look nonetheless.

The most inspiring characteristic in children is their utter disregard for torrential rain, but realising a change of scene was needed, we decamped from the kids tent to, well, the campsite, where the festival programme of events served as something to taunt you while sitting in a tepee, while the kids treated the inflatable beds as unregulated bouncy castles.

The weather improved the next day, allowing for Dave Eggers to talk about giving up writing for a year, which in light of his recent *Heroes of the Frontier* is a good thing. He is instead taking up the challenge to personally impeach the democratically elected President Trump. This is fine, although the unquestioning obedience with which his audience held up their hands as one to take a solemn oath to similarly overturn Brexit was chilling. Thankfully the good humour of Crazy Golf ensured matters did not get out of hand politically. A hole-in-one by my three-year-old, witnessed by myself, will compete as the highlight to this and any festival I've ever attended, as it did him. He spent the entire day informing anyone attempting the hole that he had managed the hole in one, before demonstrating how impossible it was to recreate.

The Curious Arts festival is a welcome addition to the festival calendar and not simply because they invited me to attend. It's chilled like the Big Chill can barely dream of these days, amongst the glorious surroundings of a manor house on talking terms with PG Wodehouse's Blandings Castle.

Meet your heroes at literary festivals.

You should never meet your heroes. Paul Newman... I was so excited about meeting him, but he turned up in shell suit bottoms, slippers, and a jumper. He was just so worn out and old. Allen Carr

Not wishing to visit Morocco and return with little more than a matchbox snake and bartering skills made instantly redundant upon landing back in the UK, I wanted to share how I met one of my literary heroes. A few years ago, I was in Marrakech for a 50th birthday, while a music/literary festival was also taking place a few miles outside the city: the rather marvelous Beat Hotel festival buzzing amongst the Bauhaus architecture of the Fellah hotel. It was as though I'd planned the serendipity myself, which obviously I hadn't, or it would not have been serendipitous.

I flew in with Booker Prize winner DBC Pierre (2003's *Vernon God Little*) and author of a wonderful book on writing called *Release the Bats*. When I say flew in with him, what I really mean is that we shared the same Easy Jet flight. His expertise at flying in for literary events was clearly evidenced by the fact that he had the front legroom seat. DBC Pierre might appear to have fallen out of San Francisco's *Northern Lights* bookshop at some point in early 1962, but he clearly knew his way round the orange riot of a budget airline website booking system to bag a good seat.

There was no appropriate opportunity to speak with him on the plane, as he spent most of it – along with everyone else - fruitlessly searching for the seat recliner button that wasn't there. Besides, who wants to be trapped in a luridly orange seat by a fan? He was also rolling a cigarette, presumable to smoke with his head down the bowl in the No Smoking toilet. I was amazed by how few other passengers apparently recognised him, but then one man's rock star is another's electrician.

I then found myself standing behind him at Passport Control. Again, this was a poor opportunity to say hello as he was endeavouring not to look like one of the 60s Beat poets likely to be refused entry to Morocco. I did however overhear him confirm 'writer' when asked about his profession scribbled on his boarding card. I glanced at my own card, but it was too late to change it from social worker. This might be a good time to admit that despite being a fellow novelist, I was not being flown in to talk; I was flying myself in to listen.

I let it go, but somehow, I overtook him and found myself outside at arrivals as he strolled out. He was wearing that I'm-confused-but-going-to-style-it-out face worn by everyone discombobulated from a flight with more hidden extras than buying a new car, whilst searching for a taxi board with their name written on it held by an unknown driver. I had him while he was down. I pounced.

I resisted informing him that I had a book about to be published for the second time before even introducing myself. I said that I knew who he was, which in hindsight sounds creepy, but he took it well. I addressed him as DBC Pierre. He kindly reduced my heavy lifting by inviting me to simply call him Pierre. He appeared genuinely delighted for me when I then told him about the imminent publication of *Unfinished Business*, appreciating the feat of novel-writing as only fellow writers (of Booker prize winning novels or self-published cat journals) truly can.

I was to see him the following day at the Beat Hotel literary event, alongside Irvine Welsh and Faber editor Lee Brackstone (whom I've discovered signed one of my favourite novels - *Haweswater* by Sarah Hall). They were knocking around the idea of 'literary outlaws', which they dismissed as 'bollocks' before demonstrating in some way how they were literary outlaws. I think they liked the concept, whilst simultaneously playing it down. I felt the line-up missed the enfant-terrible Michel Houellebecq, although Pierre was to later tell me - over

129

the euphoric crunch of Lowlife disco - that he knew Michel, and he'd probably be asleep throughout.

When Irvine Welsh asked if anyone in the audience had written a book my hand shot up. I was so near the front that my younger self would have instantly disowned me. Pierre looked at me and said 'Tom. Of course, yours is out soon, what's it called again?' '*Unfinished Business*' I replied with a clarity last seen in a demolishing ball striking abandoned buildings. 'Congratulations' said Irvine Welsh with the aforementioned genuine respect. I was one of them. Not a Booker Prize winner, or writer of the kind of zeitgeist novel precious few writers ever nail, but I was one of them, nonetheless.

There is even a photo of myself with them, alongside John Niven – another bad boy of literature – I do at least look like one of them even if my fan base and bank account would disagree. Ironically Pierre was there without a book to promote. I should have asked to take his place. He was so nice he might even have agreed. Sometimes it's good to meet your heroes. They appeared to me as writers who relish the opportunity to step from behind the page and walk and talk. They are among us.

What is it really like to be Published?

One of the other common questions people ask writers is 'What's it like being published writer? 'At least the ones who are published. You should categorically NOT ask someone unpublished this question. It is uncomfortable for everyone. 'Not yet,' is the stock answer, spoken in the sort of whisper familiar to parents being nicked for shoplifting and not wanting to wake their child. However, I've noticed correlation between getting published and an ensuing lack of interest, as though you need no encouraging, which might well be true. For no apparent reason no one asks again.

You want the truth? People who enquire about your writing don't really exist. Writers just make them up; hordes of people aching with questions about the creative processes and how they hold a tea mug. I'm unsure anyone other than fellow writers really care, but that's not going to stop us from telling you.

So, what is it really like to be a published writer? You know, beyond the fame, the adulation and the sort of life purpose familiar to intercontinental ballistic cruise missiles. It's an important question to answer, not just for writers chasing publication and curious about the climate on the sunny highlands of success, but for other published writers wishing to know how luxuriously their compatriots are living. That's the curse of writers; they have imagination, and too easily presume that others have it easy. There's this vague sense that all writers sit in book-lined rooms effortlessly knocking together lyrical bibles of prose without ever head-butting the desk as they plummet down another plot hole. If your story ever gets stuck just call it experimental and you'll probably win the Man Booker prize.

Before I was published, I spent night shifts selecting which colour I wanted my (new model) Ford Mustang in; I did not want to risk being caught short and make a panicked decision when the royalty cheque arrived, resulting in a mauve muscle car in the road outside the house. I had never considered royalties before;

131

it was all about getting published and holding the paperback in my hand, but the mind wanders once presented with possibility.

Any writer who has made it to number one in the sales chart will remember where they were when told; at least they will the first time it happened. For me it happened in the summer of 2016. I was walking around the lake in Crystal Palace park, admiring the dinosaurs as my father once had when they were the most exciting thing in 1930s south London. Their allure had faded along with their paint and indeed historical accuracy; they were modelled by their designer Benjamin Hawkins and supervised by Sir Richard Owen. The creatures that stand amongst the Jurassic trees suggest that neither had ever been on an archaeological dig.

Anyway, my phone bleeped or whatever noise they were making back then, to announce the arrival of a photo of the sales chart in Heathrow airport bookshop that a friend had sent. There it was: *The Life Assistance Agency* atop the chart, with *Harry Potter and the Cursed Child* languishing at no.2. My novel occupied the entire upper shelf of the number one position. I could not believe it. I rang my mate who was getting onto a four-hour flight, who confirmed my book was selling quicker than mini flags at a jubilee jamboree.

I was so excited I wanted to tell everyone at the same time, so I promptly posted pictures across social media like I was possessed. I was no.1 in the WHSmith sales charts and was struggling to find any sense of proportionality or humility. I mean it was a level of success nothing had prepared me for, certainly not the daydreams of literary victory. Damn, I was already worried about how to follow it up now I had more fans, at least in Heathrow, than JK Rowling. I was giddy. After losing my virginity, the safe arrival of two babies and being served a pint in a pub without ID I can't remember ever being happier. The ground disappeared as I seemingly levitated around the lake. I could have been asked for anything and I'd have said yes.

The novelty of being happy on social media was not wearing off. Instead of the political attacks there was an outpouring of pride and shared pleasure in my success from friends I'd not even seen since school. The likes were arriving quicker than I could refresh. I rang my family and planned a celebratory dinner in my own honour. The chart wall photograph was gaining more likes than the safe arrival of two babies. And then I got a text from my mate:

It had been a mistake. He had landed wherever he had in Turkey, and where I wanted him to now stay, forever, to log onto Facebook where he realised his photo was provoking a virtual party in my honour. It was now his duty to inform me that he had shifted all my books, from no.37 to the number one position in the hope it might promote it. Oh, I said, as I slipped from my literary summit, plummeting past the Sherpas, and guides, down the cliffs, and lower slopes, past base camp, past the supply lines onto the main road, all the way down to the city, where I lay slumped with disappointment in an alleyway flooded with sewage. I'm unsure if I ever recovered. I laugh about it now, but it's one of those hollow laughs you could climb into and paddle upriver in. If the truth be told, it's been upriver ever since.

However, a few months later I did get a royalty cheque, although a royalty check was more accurate. Boy, was it a reality check. It's seldom you witness dreams crash to the ground in a fireball of crushed dreams so easily, but not here. An email notifying me of the royalty cheque coincided with being on holiday and the children begging for an ice cream. I looked at the amount, which was the first and, to date, last time, I was paid by my publisher. I rubbed my eyes. It was a third of what I earned per month as a social worker. The publisher had made clear this was the yearly cheque. Well, the offspring got a shock too. In the flush of financial windfall, they got an ice cream and in order not to feel left out, I bought myself a frisbee. How I wish that this story wasn't true. The Mustang would have to wait. Probably forever.

133

Having completed the sequel to the Life Assistance Agency I found myself back in a familiar place. Not having a book to write feels like having trousers without pockets; it's hard to know what to do with your hands. For most writers scribbling is a glorified hobby, and the greatest motivator to finishing a novel is the opportunity to discard old drafts, notes and research that prevents the cupboard under the stairs from opening fully.

Being published changes your focus, but the world doesn't stop. Planes that you're a day late to the airport to catch don't wait on the airstrip wondering where you are – as I once discovered at the cost of replacement flight home. And worries that the thud of royalties on the doormat might wake the neighbours are put to rest when it barely wakes you, despite sleeping on the doormat in anticipation.

It's quite fun looking for writers. They're easy to spot. They have a distant look in their eyes. They're the ones clutching their emotional support squirrels tight enough to attract attention from the RSPCA. Most annoyingly you still have to tell people that you've written a book. Stephen King has always suggested that you must write, write, write, or read, read, read, but what he neglected to say was promote, promote, promote. Even he still does it, mainly by slagging off Trump on Twitter, but still. The worst thing is being asked to rewrite something by your boss in your day job because it's not good enough. 'd'you know who I *really* am? 'bubbles to your lips like water breaching a weir, before you think better of it as the reason for that distant look in your eye might be explained.

To be honest not much changes after publication, although you might legitimately consider yourself an author as opposed to a writer, at least you can until someone enquires what the difference is. It's almost the same life as you had before, I don't just mean the ignominy of having to take out your own rubbish bags or occasionally having to answer the trade door in the west wing. It's the same as before but without a £45,000 Ford

Mustang spurring you on, and a permanent public record of missed pelling* mistakes.

*spelling.

Writing the second novel

A year after I posted the manuscript of my debut novel to my publisher, I was itching to write The End to its sequel. This in despite of the knowledge that nothing actually happens once you do. A fleeting kick of achievement at best. I had intended to capture the moment on a webcam but watching an author working is akin to observing someone looking for something without knowing what it is that they have lost. Perhaps this is most people's relationship with purpose in life. A novel is similar to finding a goal in life. You do not plan to fail, but you fail to plan. It's all very well watching motivational clips on YouTube, damn it's better for you than the poison of the news, but you still need a goal. Watching a writer typing out The End isn't worth two years of previous footage. There might be a smile, there might be a lean back in the chair, who knows. It certainly isn't a triple backflip into the stalls of the home stand. But what you can hear is the ball hitting the net.

There's a hesitancy as you claw your final yards to the summit. The conclusion to the creative spark that preserved in its need to hang flesh on imagination is barely mentioned. Instead, the end is in sight is the kind of rallying cry familiar to Edwardian explorers (if there's any left) before they noticed another perilous crevice of 800 feet to be negotiated before supper using nothing but frayed ropes, crampons and battered pipes clamped between gritted teeth. I remember the rush and imminent regret as I viewed the remaining virgin ground left before the sequel's end. It was a few thousand words; the end was in sight.

I wrote the second book at a speed better associated with Londoners pouncing on vacated rush hour Northern line seats, which is my own fault for leaving such obvious potential for a follow-up to the first. And that's good advice. Just as it's advisable to end a scene halfway through, sometimes mid-sentence, as opposed to when the door closes. It can be too challenging to open it again. Similarly, it is sensible to always leave a novel with an ending open enough to reverse a Massey Ferguson combine harvester through sideways blindfolded.

As we have already established, being a writer provokes questions, and not only 'can you pay back that tenner yet?' There is a misconception that you must roll out of bed into the type of sense of purpose causing bidding wars on E-bay. Most writers are rolling in it, but only if 'it' refers to misplaced punctuation, unfillable plot holes and underused characters. Oh, and biscuit crumbs. I was delighted that readers of the first book were asking for a sequel until I realised it meant I needed to write one. I was still rolling out of bed and finding nothing but my slippers (on a good day), but the urge was there; the desire to provide a story with some air.

Some asked if writing the second novel was easier. In a way it was, but only like the second girlfriend (or whatever it is we're calling them these days) feels the same, yet completely different. Much like those inept explorers, the endeavour of writing a novel is started through the wrong end of a telescope, where a distant and idealised destination appears. Although most of the time you're arguing with automated fake Twitter accounts about the wisdom of Croydon's tram system.

It's always too early for saying it's going well; even to yourself. It's easy to verge from rehearsing Not the Booker Prize acceptance speech, to calling Apple support desperately requesting how to retrieve deleted manuscripts from the computer's hard drive that may not even have been there in the first place. The best advice is to enjoy the first draft if you can, because you'll never be as playful with it again; it is for you alone. The second draft is not yours. It is for the reader. It's tightening the screws on what already exists. You're out of the picture. It's all about the clipboard and kicking the tyres for hardness. But the first draft? Well, that's the sandpit.

What's so good about sequels?

Most authors will be familiar with having finished writing a novel. Sometimes it's completed for as long as 24 hours before another rewrite is underway. That's fine. That's how novels are written, but when my 79,000 words of *Unfinished Business* had been sent to the publisher, I was prone to reflect on how I had got there. There were to be no more late-night edits to be undone in the morning. The bound-up proofs would be defying any desire to make changes. It had been a long time since a friend suggested I write a short film and I came up with the idea of a retired 80s wrestler who morphed into a character even bigger than Ricky 'Nasty 'Bashcraft, or Giant Haystacks, which consisted of the chopping boards on which the novel weas diced.

Just as its proprietor Scott Wildblood needed a wingman *The Life Assistance Agency* now had a companion, as there's nothing worse than a novel sitting alone, full of friends and enemies bouncing off the inside covers with nowhere to go. It found itself with a sequel. The journey that began as a film script had become a novel. It was like driving the wrong way down the inspirational highway, the opposite of turning base metal into gold. I had turned the promise of pounds into pennies. Of course, now I'm adapting it for a TV series at the bequeath of nobody. I'm banking on Netflix needing content.

What is it with sequels? We love them. We spend two hours watching one film and want another one the same. They're like cake or olives. Perhaps that is why I wrote a sequel to the Life Assistance Agency. I suspect I was also motivated by the fact that the characters had unfinished business, and I don't just mean pulling up the handbrake in the fast lane leading in the wrong direction. That the first ever "talkie" sequel to 1927's *The Jazz Singer* made more money in 1928 than the original, despite being called *The Singing Fool*, was deeply encouraging and can be held responsible for 1993's *Look Who's Talking Now*. Yes, I believe it was the pets.

138

People love sequels, although none more than Sylvester Stallone. What is it with him and sequels? Rambo is indestructible, and although I'm not complaining, Rocky could carry on indefinitely, as the recent lane-switch of the Creed franchise proves. However, it has also resulted in *Expendables 4*; that's four movies of the OAP gym away-day spent competing in testosterone levels, chewing cigars and the repetitive lifting of M2 Browning machine guns. At this rate he'll be following up *Stop, or my Mum will Shoot*.

Thus, taking the jab from Stallone, it was a long time ago when I assured that Random House commissioning editor that I had a meticulously planned trilogy of novels about Ben, a young-ish man whose sole skill is involving himself in dead end jobs, at least until he reacquaints himself with Scott Wildblood and his Life Assistance Agency, which he spends the first novel joining and this second novel regretting. Like most jobs he'd ever held he was unenthusiastic. That's my character I mean. The commissioning editor clearly loved his job as he was the only person in the UK not hoping to get published. Apparently, he had given up that dream, and you could see it. He walked with the lightness of a man not carrying the weight of a novel-in-progress. He negotiated life having declined the opportunity to chase elusive dreams. That reminds me, I used to bump into a very successful literary agent with such frequency that it verged on accidental stalking and she had also given up writing after realising she was shit. She was a woman liberated from her own personal literary ambition and it showed.

And so, the sequel started – spoiler alert – with the Life Assistance Agency stuck in a lift, and I wish I could report that their slick professionalism improves from there, but Ben was so eager to avoid further entanglement with the angel-calling nonsense that he gratefully agreed to writing the biography of a pop star quietly planning his comeback in rural Sussex.

It was on publication of the sequel that I too lost my ride. I wasn't thrown. I simply found it impossible to look the horse in the eye. Something had happened. It would appear that reality of publication for me was utterly stupefying. It's hard to keep your shoulder to the wheel when your publisher shows as much interest in self-promotion as someone rapidly exiting the British Museum having accidentally set its ground floor toilets alight. That wafer-thin line between the writer and protagonist vanished and I felt as lost as Ben. Any self-respecting HR department would have closed down all Word documents and escorted me off the premises.

As we know, there is a danger to sequels; like a kiss or a hotdog, the second is not guaranteed to be as good as the first. To every Studio 54 there's a studio 45, where in lieu of Jade Jagger riding a white horse bareback at 2am there is someone who's had too many and is pogoing about the dancefloor on the tattered remains of a hobby horse found in the skip outside while singing *I will survive* through a traffic cone. Well, I hope *Unfinished Business* is as good as the title. The people who've read it declare it better than the first, that it's an *Empire Strikes Back* or *Godfather 2*, albeit with a slightly smaller promotional budget and less demand. They might even be right, but it soon became apparent that my sequel lacked the audience of the first. It had all the traction of climbing a ferry side using nothing but your hands. There was no Fresh Talent award this time. There was no cake with my book cover replicated in icing. If it wasn't for my frequent emails to my publisher then they might have forgotten me entirely.

And there was worse to come. What I found loitering on the far side of the sequel, head bowed down, face obscured, was the dreaded writer's block. I had ideas for the concluding book, but if no one was reading the first two, not even my publisher, then where was the impetus to write a third? The story had found its tracks; yet had lost its locomotion. What happens when the music stops? You write a book on writing. You bring up children. You build a shed or take up surfing, but you're still a writer. You can still snip the chord to that humdrum habitual existence in an instant with fingers on the keys, or pen to paper. Writing is free associating, it is seeing what unfurls, and which corners find light that would otherwise be left dark and unloved. There's a desire to complete the trilogy. I want my characters to find some peace.

Importance of Location

Following the publication of *Unfinished Business*, I was kindly asked to write a feature on the importance of location in fictional writing for Trip Fiction. What a buzz that was. Who doesn't enjoy a strong location that you will never visit in a novel It takes out all the legwork. Mind you, I didn't fall upon my location from the other side of the undergrowth while fetching a football. I wish I had. It was all there at the end of daydreaming about road trips and train rides. It was set in a place I had little hope of ever visiting.

So many novels perfectly encapsulate place, sometimes even better than the location itself. The Prague of Milan Kundera, or the London of Patrick Hamilton are somehow more real than the actual cities themselves. To read a novel can result in visiting the place in which it is set and be disappointed. I imagine this is particularly pronounced for *Game of Thrones* fans visiting Winterfell at Castle Ward in Northern Ireland only to discover it was a composite, with the other half being Down Castle in Scotland. No one likes to feel short changed.

To be honest I do question whether some writers have actually visited the places they set their novels, and I don't just mean Arthur C Clarke not having been to Thalassa. There are novels such as both Lawrence Osborne's *Beautiful Animals* and John Fowles' *The Magus* that are as inseparable from the Greek islands as L.A. is to Raymond Chandler's *The Big Sleep*. If they haven't been to those places, then they have certainly earned their dough.

My favourite moment as a published writer was when I was asked online about locations in *the Life Assistance Agency*. It was by a fan. I'm hesitant to describe her as a fan, but not enough to neglect describing her as such. She asked if there was indeed an abandoned police station in London's Marble Arch. Yes, I replied, somewhat dumbstruck at the clear *evidence* that she had read my novel. She hadn't just claimed to have read it but was asking about specific details that no one else had. I was pleased enough with being the only person alive, other than the retired police officers, knowing there had once been a police station in Marble Arch, but now I could share it publicly. She was nervous, which endeared her even further to me. I overcame my own nerves and confirmed that it was indeed in existence, and that discovering it had given me the sort of rush familiar to punters waving winning stubs at horserace finishing lines. It was the sort of location you couldn't make up.

I love to find interesting places and then think of some way to shoehorn them into a novel. It is always place first. I did this with *Unfinished Business*. I was reading about deserted theme parks as you do when you have loads of more important stuff to be doing, and realised I needed one in my novel. When I say need, it was more of a gratuitous desire than need, but what's the difference? I then aligned the plot to justify the sort of ruin porn people fly drones over Chernobyl for.

The Internet took minutes to discover the *Dogpatch* rustic theme park in Arkansas that fell to its financial knees in the 80s and crawled onwards before finally surrendering to its debtors in 1993. It was based on Al Capp's hillbilly themed *Li'l Abner* comic strip (nope, me neither), and tapped into an appetite for American hillbillies and trout fishing that didn't exist outside the owners' business model. To think folk were paying to walk through fake dilapidated buildings in the US while UK teenagers were loitering around mobile phones in motorway service station car parks to confirm the location of a rave is staggering.

Anyway, there was *Barney Barnsmell's Skunk-Works, Rotten Raplhie's Rick-O-Shay Riffle Range*, a rollercoaster called *Earthquake McGoon's Brain Rattler* and you could feed mechanical pigs rubbish, or trash as it's known over the pond. I mean what's not to like, although I'm guessing this gave Trip Advisor reviews at the time an open goal. The best place for the business model was probably inside the mechanical pigs. But as a setting it was perfect, everyone likes spooky theme parks, apart from Scooby Doo, and it played a crucial role in the new novel. I endeavour to visit the places I set my writing, but in this instance, it was hard to justify travelling 4, 500 miles to see (or smell) rusting remains of mechanical skunks. I'd like to go sometime, or just pay a local drone owner to fly one over the park.

Unfinished Business is not set solely in the US, which in light of me not having visited is for the best. Leafy Sussex and the chalky edge of England were far easier to investigate. I was however a little alarmed that the drive to Beachy Head was much longer than expected, as it appeared to have moved to the far side of Eastbourne from where I expected. Four hours later I fell gratefully out of the car, thankfully not too near the 600-foot drop.

I'd like *Unfinished Business* to be synonymous with the landscape of Sussex in the same way as Newfoundland in Annie Proulx's *Shipping News*, but if it simply provokes a reader to ask if the deserted theme park in Arkansas is real then I'll be happy enough with saying yes. One day I'll visit and see if the locations of pivotal events in the novel match up to how I described them (although I'm very happy for feedback on Amazon reviews so long as it's not too cutting). But above all, there's a part of me that believes all the events happened in a fictional place that almost exists, a bit like the comic strip it was based upon that no one has heard of.

Delude yourself.

If you can delude yourself then you can be a writer. All writers begin deluded, and success only confirms the illusion.

We all delude ourselves. We cut past traffic and take the inside lane on the Hyde Park roundabout and we're instantly Nikki Lauda. Walk up to the bar and get served first and we're Jimmy Dean of the first order. Catch a teacup before it hits the floor and we momentarily believe in our ability to stop time. And it's not often you want to do that, not since the era of national Lockdowns.

We spend a lot of time denouncing delusions as dangerous, fantastical and misleading, but when it comes to writing it's crucial. If you can squint to glimpse a rural 1950s car garage, with its mechanic wiping oily hands on his blue overalls, before rolling himself a cigarette as the sun catches the corrugated iron of his makeshift office that he intends to make more permanent but never quite gets round to it, then you can squint and see yourself as a writer. That's the first move on the writing board. You can win. You can be successful. Let's face it in our Western institutions there are no winners anymore, identifying someone as a loser is offensive, although that's not to say there *aren't* winners.

Winners means there are losers, and it would seem that we have to protect our darlings from failure; they're not robust enough. Well, that's certainly guaranteed if you're protected from losing meaning your first experience of failure is as a 24-year old graduate thrust into the workplace where the ancient hunting trails still echo with their thrill of the chase and the fastest, of fresh blood and the marrow of achievement. A childhood wearing gloves leads to a soft-handed adulthood. We might tell them that no one goes in bare-knuckle anymore, but they do, every time; the gloves are still off, it's just harder to see. It's tooth and claw like it has always been. Regardless as to how thickly you plaster over our old ways there will always be winners and losers.

With writing success isn't winning. Not really. I mean, it's nice, but it's not the picture. It is not the taking part that counts either, not really. It's actually completing something; something for yourself. Any lame schmuck can begin something. It is completion that strikes the outfield so hard that faces look up, but most importantly your own. If you complete a novel, you can face yourself. If you can tell yourself a fully wrapped up and roughly comprehensible story, then you can beat yourself; all those doubts and proclivities to take the easier less challenging route are shattered. You've won.

The importance of imagining yourself as a writer is as important as imagining your characters. And don't be distracted. Use everything and everyone. Pluck what you need from the air; it's all there. There's a school of thought that prescribes the idea that when asked to do a laborious task, do it so poorly that you are never asked again. While there's some mileage in this, it is inadvisable to apply it to vocational pursuits. I learned this during the summer holidays from school. I was seventeen and needed money. I forget for what, probably to fill the car with petrol, but it was clearly crucial at the time, crucial enough to start offering my services out locally as a gardener.

There was a local resident whom once I saw the size of their colossal hedge, I realised had been waiting for some fresh blood to undertake the mammoth task. I'm certain to this day there was no gardener within a twenty-mile radius willing to tackle it with a barge pole, or even an extendable hedge trimmer. An extendable hedge trimmer, or rather the lack of one, was to haunt me for the next three weeks. I visited to size up the laurel monstrosity that loomed over their house and the road like a developing rain cloud. It was challenging but do-able I said, aware that cutting the hedge down to size would comparatively quadruple the size of their house, and probably even its resale value.

146

Then we rounded a corner and they showed me the rest of it. It was a galleon of a hedge, a true man 'o war. There were nests in there established during the reign of James 1st. I agreed to the job at the sort of rate union officials would have thrust a clipboard in the way of and arranged to start the following day. I had shears and by lunchtime there was nothing to show for three hours work, multiple blisters, and arms that had lost all ability to move their hands. The hedge was invincible.

My afternoon was spent with flies and wasps divebombing my sweating face and ears, which I defended against by tying my shirt over my head, meaning I could barely see what I was trimming. Not that it made any difference. I finished early and spent the night dreaming of an extendable hedge trimmer, which for a seventeen-year-old boy is a first. I finished the job after four weeks. I stood back and admired the hedge, which in hindsight would have been justified in claiming 'it's not what I asked for. ' A flaming hatchback losing control on the corner before exploding within its depths might have done a neater job. But I deluded myself into thinking it was a job well done. I wasn't cutting a hedge. I was slashing the vines that led to the abandoned temple of bloom.

And now I've used it. Right here and now. I had forgotten all about it until a moment ago, yet it was there, sloshing around in my head. The sort of the memory that is shapeless until you write it down. It's all there. Delude yourself and it might become real. Find yourself.

Are Writers past their sell by date?

One of the problems of being a writer, apart from the frown, and that the last thing you wrote being a phone number for a recommended plumber, is the fear you're only as good as the last thing you wrote. Although parsley, butter and cheese might be significant at the time, they offer poor legacy when the Southbank Show or Sky Arts call to document the writer at work. The Southbank Show was taken off air in the Middle Ages so the likelihood of their interest in my shopping list is unlikely, but it's important to be prepared all the same. After all I've had a ten pence piece in my pocket since I got the Scout's Nuclear Winter Survival badge. I sometimes wonder if a childhood overshadowed by the imminent possibility of spending two years beneath a reinforced kitchen table with your immediate family and mutating family pet whilst listening to sinister public announcements as the world collapses amongst radioactive flames may have had an impact on my generations' level of risk assessment. We were the last generation smiling up from beneath home-cut pudding bowl hair as opposed to bicycle helmets.

Deciding to be a writer is a result of particularly poor cost/risk/benefit analysis. Research has suggested that only 10% of writers earn a living from their endeavours. There's little achievement in the royalties check. The thrill of being a writer is like being wired up to a medical drip delivering tight succinct lines that will change the world (or at the least your day; until lunchtime). The only problem being that you are also the administrator and drug manufacturer. That means for every laser-guided metaphor there's also asparagus and toilet roll. And refusing to write shopping lists won't help, that simply results in wandering around the supermarket like an overwhelmed time-traveller. You might have seen people looking baffled in the cereal aisle; they're writers with their mind firmly on the last thing they wrote as opposed to what they should have; was it oaty cereal, or cereal oats? But there's something else.

Tesco have recently announced that they're scrapping sell-by dates on fruit and veg because people don't understand them. What are customers incapable of reading dates doing in the supermarket and how did they even get there? Please don't tell me by car. People incapable of comprehending food sell-by-dates should NOT be allowed in supermarkets, much less on the road, unless they are driven. In fact, anyone whose intellect is challenged by dates on, say dates, should be stopped at the door by DVLA and stripped of their licence before they reach their car. Unless they're writers of course. It's exactly this sort of thing, along with royalties that carves those frowns upon writers' faces. If people can't read sell-by-dates on fruit, then what hope is there for your carefully arranged words being read in comprehensible order?

There are still some readers out there and it's their good fortune that writers don't know where they live. They are the birds on a tree planted so long ago that the author can barely recall digging in the seed. The reader is a mythical creature to the writer, particularly when you're weighing up the wisdom of a car chase versus a backgammon challenge between the main protagonists. I had only flirted with the idea of a sequel until a reader asked if there was to be one. If only I had realised the internal contract being signed with myself as I nodded my head.

I agreed on the spot, as though a Wembley packed with fans were chanting for it, before writing the idea on my hand to remind me. It's those readers who make writers momentarily content with those written lines; that they might live on in some way. And it gives confidence in being able to write a shopping list without compromising their artistic integrity, besides it's worth not getting lost in the cereal aisle if you get home sooner to write.

Yes, writing is a risk. But so is life. Life without risk is unquestionably appealing for the duration of a hangover, but the lack of novelty would soon pale. Living is more important than Life. And if you think writing is old fashioned, give Andy

149

Hamilton a go. He's written a book, *Longhand*, in handwriting. Yes, in the 21st century. It makes typed books appear positively modern. Thank you, Andy. Although surely the word handwriting is unnecessary; with what else are you going to write? Perhaps handwriting was competing with a craze for footwriting at the time and thankfully prevailed, although to be fair my signature might be more illegible if written with my feet.

How to buy books.

Well, here's the real trick. There are invisible dark arts at play in how a book falls into your hands. From those misty sixth form days, when you wandered around with Proust under your arm, hoping the girls might rip themselves from the footballers' embrace and glance in your direction, to reading the grown-up covers of Harry Potter on the train. While Proust was ineffective as a sex magnet, I do know that he considered a glass of chilled beer as a more reliable source of pleasure than lovemaking, so I at least learned something important. There's probably always been more reading done in bedrooms than shagging, so we don't have to feel bad about that either. I know someone who only reads novels in bed. They do not allow autobiographies into the bedroom; they are read downstairs in full view of the family. Perhaps they don't want all that dirty laundry aired near the clean bed linen. I'm unclear where their stance is on sex in the bedroom.

The proven method in buying books to walk past a bookshop absolutely determined not to go in. And then go in. I've walked a few hundred yards further on from a book shop quietly congratulating myself for having not gone in, before turning back and entering. They are alluring things bookshops, so full of promise. I'm not sure it's entirely based upon the content of what they sell; it's not just books, but what they represent, and books represent time. Implicit in buying a book is the idea that you will have time to read it. And if you do you will travel through time, to places unseen and thoughts unsaid. Bookshops sell time.

The very idea of a book is delicious. Sitting down (yes, we're back there again), and immediately appearing as though in a lifestyle advert. You know the ones. Some quietly attractive woman folding her legs beneath her, as she sips a perfect hot chocolate on the sofa and opens a book. In reality it would be at this point that she spills the drink all over the cream upholstery as the doorbell rings with a deliveryman asking if she wouldn't mind taking a parcel for next door, which she trips over for weeks every time she leaves the house. So, is reading the suspension of time? Perhaps so, there's certainly a time warp in bookshops. You lose sense of time. i.e., the discrepancy between the amount of time you have available to read and the number of books you buy to read. There must be a word for this level of utterly baseless optimism, yet it's utterly charming. In so many ways books represent the optimism of the human spirit. There's no reader with a to-read pile that isn't double their body weight.

Books in bookshops are like that extra pint in the pub. It won't matter, but my God it does in the morning. One more book won't hurt, and just *look* at the cover. The pretty cover art twinkles like pier lights in the coastal dusk and pulls a sad face if you walk away. That's what returns you to the bookshop, it's all those gorgeous covers; the ones whose sole purpose in life is to commandeer your attention. How can you live with yourself if it fails in its sole life purpose?

Too often a novel sounds better than it is, as though it's regrettable that the author failed to read their own back cover blurb before starting the book. In fact, a good trick in writing is to consider the lacuna between your expectations of a published novel and the reality; and write the book you hoped it would be yourself.

I've always thought it was a good idea for a TV show to have two famous writers given the same plot and ask them to write their version of the story. The show could follow the writing process as an insight into the variety of approaches, and how much idiosyncrasies individuals bring to the same remit. It could be called not the Voice but the Word. Oh, we've already been there. This sounds like a good idea on paper until the idea of an observational documentary on writers is not exactly packed with formula 1 thrills or the drama of heavyweight boxing. If they had the character of Mary Shelley or were tumbling out of bars and embracing free love then it might be worth watching, but on the other hand this has probably been covered by Newcastle: uncovered. Weekly episodes of writers mooching around farmer's markets or taking the dog for a walk and swearing at the weather when they should be writing is hardly mainstream entertainment.

Filming someone buying books would be even less entertaining, albeit revealing. Your choice of books reveals a great deal about you, or rather reveals a great deal of how you want people to see you. We all do it, or at least have done it. I knew someone who put their Virago and Penguin classics at eye height on their bookshelf, leaving lesser 'considered '(which is a sort of academic word people use when nibbling the arm of their reading glasses in a thoughtful manner) at a lower level. Mind you, kudos to her for not hiding the pulp fiction under the bed. This is exactly the snobbery needing to be put aside when you're in a bookshop. This is where you can indulge your private interest in hot air balloons and pet tigers, and if there aren't any books on those, then damn well write one. Shoot for the moon, and if you miss you may just hit one of those magnificent flying machines.

How to Survive bad reviews

Every time I read 'Pride and Prejudice' I want to dig her up and beat her over the skull with her own shinbone. Mark Twain.

They say a bad review lasts a week and a good one barely an hour. Never think this is untrue. No matter how successful you are, a bad review can burrow into your confidence like determined woodworm. It makes you wish you'd always gone for your second-choice word and not the first, which is good advice actually. The sort you read only once when you've already completed writing a book.

There is so much focus upon writing, on the tips and tricks, that too frequently the real skill is neglected. And that is the art of disallowing poor feedback or bad reviews from ruining your day, and your ENTIRE BLOODY LIFE AND EVERYTHING THAT HAS LED TO THAT DISASTROUS MOMENT, which is pretty much what neighbours heard when I read my first 2-star review of the Life Assistance Agency on Amazon. There had been 5-star reviews but I'd not seen them.

Ironically writers chase reviews because it helps with algorithms and sales, although no one has yet provided a coherent answer as to how this works without ending up sounding like a conspiracy theorist. And what reviews fail to help with is your mental stability. Or do they? What writers really want is GOOD reviews, but then that's the risk. That is what writing is all about. It's increasing the risk of someone calling you a twat. If you can live with that then press on. If not, well, perhaps it's better to step away. Not that you'll be safe, they will find another means with which to call you names.

Unlike the Internet another great thing about bookshops is that people don't wander around the establishment marking everything out of ten stars, or writing pithy comments about lead character's dress sense, or how the acceleration of a Saab 900 is actually twice as slow as you described it, unless it's been fitted

154

with a larger carburetor. You can slag books off to the proprietor, of the shop, although I suspect they hire people to take the public flak. I'm not even convinced you have to pay people to work in a bookshop; they're kind of born to it. Even if you do provide your unrequested book review the staff will pull the blank expression of a priest taking confession in case there's other customers nearby intending to purchase said novel. I once spent a good ten minutes, or at least I suspect it felt like that for the owner, slagging off a Jonathan Coe novel, while he watched another customer put it down and walk out the shop. Mind you, it was a bit crap.

The best place to hear feedback to your own writing is in the pub, whilst if not holding a pint then certainly within reach of one. You can drain it if necessary, and then smash the critic over the head with the jug. Most annoyingly the smug contentment of good reviews is too easily smeared by a single bad one. A poor review sticks like a squished iced bun to the shoe of creativity. But writers are resilient. It is why they hide away from life in rooms with cats warming their knees, or dogs their feet. It is why they never answer the phone.

Writers have to be tough; or learn to be. It is an essential part of being a writer and pursuing goals; just look at Ethan Hunt in Mission Impossible. He's your lead on this. Dreams need reality. Dreamers sail into the abyss with smudged notes scribbled on the back of their hand, a well-practised autograph and complete lack of objectivity or a map. They frequently discover that emerging into the cold light of subjective reality can be a shocking experience. What d'you mean no one wants to read a steam punk caravan road trip fitness manual? Are you really writing a novel featuring a BAME character as a white man? Stories that are born in one head hoping to live on in another require a strong and sturdy bridge between. Make it strong enough and there's no need to ask for consent. Alice lives in Wonderland, but also in heads that have never even read Lewis Carroll's book. Fling the story hard enough, with jetpack blast, and it will stick; never question that.

If there is one thing that writing teaches an author, other than how easily the semi-colon can be misused and how gleefully people love to point that out to you, it is to prevail. Writing gives purpose to an aimless day and teaches resilience. When you have published a book that's had as much promotion as the French national cricket team and some smart arse points out that the story is weak, the characters underwhelming and the cover design a car crash of font lorries jack-knifing across the calligraphy highway, it is necessary to be thick skinned. And resilience is a useful skill to have in life, one seemingly lacking in some parts of contemporary society. Creativity is sticking your neck out shouting an invitation to chop your head off. No one becomes an artist without taking blows for their artistry. And sometimes it's needed. Critical comments guide the hand of the fragile ego, if it allows them to. Showing people who you are is always risky, but it's cold in the shadows if you stay there too long.

I did have one bad review that made me laugh. In a good way, not in a kind of creepy world-domination kind of a way. It was so funny that I momentarily wondered if it was funnier than the novel itself. They said it had been less fun than hanging up their washing, but that they were a clown. I quickly shock myself loose of that one. The real skill is not to shout, fuck it and start throwing stuff at the floor. We think we are as tough as the Incredible Hulk yet remember how thin-skinned he is. And let's not forget how wrong reviewers can be. I once reviewed The The playing at Brixton, and after reading some of the glowing press reviews, I wondered if I'd been at a different gig. There was no mention of the muddily boring sound and a sea of bald heads waiting for *Uncertain Smile* so they could go home. It was full of nosed-up music industry none of whom had paid for their ticket and it showed. Free things are valueless; there's no investment. And never forget how some writers and artists are such media darlings that they repel bad reviews like magnets.

Schools and college are a good place to experience rejections. From girls, from boys, from the football team, ok, and from the rugby, cricket, swimming, bridge, badminton and even debating team. It was only recently that I realised I had spent most of my school education punching holes in handouts for ring binders and reinforcing the holes with tiny polo-like stickers. These were handouts never to see the light of day again. It was at some point during my first term at university that I realised hole reinforcing was not a transferable life skill and got a bar job instead. At least I would have had I not failed the interview. Yes, to a bar job. I pretend that didn't happen. But experiencing rejection is a life skill. It builds armour to make you stronger. It makes the praise more real. And it makes you better at writing, or painting, or bar work; whatever it is you think you're good at, you can always be better. Find your fire. The desire is in there. Let your ambition fan the flames.

What's the best thing about being a writer?

There is nothing to writing. All you do is sit down at a typewriter and bleed. - Ernest Hemingway

Time to dig deep here. In light of the number of new year resolutions including the intention to write a novel there must be something appealing about the writerly life, but what is so bloody great about it? I wonder if some people confuse writing with reading. It's hard to understand why. Reading is a strangely magical experience, which tingles otherwise untouched parts of you, like sausage rolls without the guilt. Reading is the ease of a polished parquet on the cruise ship. Writing on the other hand is the challenge of typing whilst simultaneously wringing your hands and swearing quietly. Writing is the laying of the new parquet floor in rough seas, whilst seasick. You discover the distinction between the two the hard way.

Perhaps it's despair at such sudden disappearance of chocolate yule logs from shops after Christmas that drives people into the collective arms of manuals and writing groups, or perhaps it's to emulate all those fantastic books half read during the festive season. But don't be rash, those rather delicious afternoons with nothing to do but eat chocolates and dream characters to life tend not to extend beyond 2nd January when your boss starts questioning your performance in areas you've not heard of since you researched them to put on your CV. It's also too easy to base a lead character on members of your family over the Christmas period and being sued for libel can rather set the creative process back, not to mention getting no gifts next year.

However, January is an effective time to undertake new projects. TV has shot its best with Christmas Specials and no one goes out, other than those poor souls with January birthdays. There's something about winterly grey days that suggest no one is doing anything other than wondering why only the British eat crumpets. A wonderful Irish friend of mine recently revealed she had never heard of them. I mean how is that possible? They are however better suited to winter, when you need as much insulation against the ennui as baked goods can offer. The darkness asks too many questions, as does writing. And let's not even discuss the national Lockdowns where initial enthusiasm at working from home seeped slowly from our social media updates like armbands deflating at the end of a holiday.

A story is a puzzle with pieces only the writer can cut. It's not like real life. Real life is like sitting behind a giraffe at the theatre; you're there but you can't see anything and you're wondering how the hell it got through the foyer in the first place. Writing, like reading, pitches you into the action. You can't miss a thing. Being a writer does not mean you're always asking world-changing questions (you're certainly not answering them), but you are at least hoping to get points for trying. You might be wondering how to rewire a light switch, or simply enquiring why people attach eyelashes to their car's headlamps. I mean what's that about? As if we're not busy enough already we're now volunteering to manicure our bloody cars. Does the car eventually ask if it can use the rest of your make-up and borrow your favourite dress? I mean who wants their Nissan Micra looking more glamorous than they are? And trust me, I've witnessed this on two different occasions.

Anyway, I stray from my originally precise intentions (I did have them I promise). People often ask what's so good about writing. Actually, they don't, because they are people I have fabricated so I can tell you. The reason people never ask what's so good about writing is because they're too furious at you for not taking the rubbish out or leaving no petrol in the car and don't give two hoots if calling your attention to this this disturbs the creative process. Some people are vaguely impressed that you're attempting to write the novel, but they don't live with you. And yes, that's the novel that we all apparently have in us. Physiology has long-since proven this not to be the case, yet the idea persists. I wonder where that concept began? In the pub probably.

It is bleeding obvious what's so appealing about writing; it's finding a plate of flapjack crumbs in your bed at lunchtime. The problem is that everyone is doing this during the holidays, which partly leads them to conclude they can write too. Getting out the house is the best thing about being a writer. A walk becomes research, a film is inspiration, a song provokes interpretative dance, and a nap inspires a poem. Sitting in public to hear how people talk is always useful:

'A neighbour had a cataract operation. '
'Oh, so did a friend. Did they have to stay really still?'

I mean what kind of a response is that? No, the intricate operation involving the removal of the natural lens of the eye and replaced with an intraocular lens via an intricate incision was carried out by a surgeon on a rollerblades! You cannot make this stuff up; it's priceless. Perhaps that's the challenge of Lockdowns on the creative process. All there is to do is watch TV, read books, homeschool and avoid zoom 'parties'. Subsequently everything you're exposed to has already been honed down to the contents of your fridge.

It takes a long time to master the strange process of writing. Just as the quickest method to encourage the arrival of a bus is to light a cigarette, the best way to write is to do something else entirely. The less practical it is to write, the more inspired you will be. Rock climbing is always very effective, particularly if you've left your pen at the bottom of the cliff. Or ideally be on the edge of something monumental and be interrupted. This worked a treat for Coleridge, who blamed the visitor from Porlock for disturbing his poem Kubla Khan. The reason for the home visit remains unclear – I do wonder if it was a social worker - but it'd better have been a good one if you've just interrupted a literary masterpiece, but it was probably just the 18th century equivalent of a postman asking if Coleridge might sign for a neighbour's parcel. We will never know if he was actually interrupted, or had opted for a snooze, with the intention of finishing his masterpiece later and woke up having lost his thread, resorting to making up a visitor from Porlock, to enable him to live with costliest snooze ever. To be fair, arranging to be interrupted is not the greatest challenge to writers, most actively pursue it, but not the serious ones.

The people of Porlock in Somerset have never recovered their reputation as interrupters of literary masterpieces. But what authors need is more readers. Reading changes your world, even briefly, and without readers writers are little more than spindles spinning without purpose in the dark.

Some more thoughts on Writing block

Writing about a writer's block is better than not writing at all. - Charles Bukowski

What awful timing, or perhaps it's related. When my second novel *Unfinished Business* was published, I was struck down by what felt like something I was reluctant to name. No, not a STD, but writer's block. Despite a launch party that included four Spanish women speaking not one word of English arriving to buy a signed copy of the novel for one of their brothers, I'm looking at the novel with the sense it was a fluke; never to be repeated.

I can't recall if I've written about writer's block before, I must've blocked it out, which is exactly the sort of lame joke that suggests it's time to step away from the keyboard and do something else. Anything. Just stop writing. Mind you writers are incapable of much else, unless it's the dismantling of a pre-industrial wool looms for research purposes.

I think I have avoided writing about writer's block because like swerving descriptions of Volvos it's best to pretend some things don't exist, alongside bell-bottomed jeans, Kinder Eggs and depression. Yet it does, and it might not sound much, but for writers it's like a carpenter losing the ability to saw straight or recognise a lathe. If you're not writing then what are you? I touched on this in my novel, where a pop star struggles to compensate for failing in his dreams of dominating the music world by swimming daily lengths of his swimming pool, which if shaped like a guitar might have simultaneously exercised his ego, but it never really answered the question. If you have spent your life holding a dream, it's hard to know what to replace it with.

There's something deft about writing. Being a writer is the ability to switch the reader from the first-class cabin of a transatlantic flight, to ordering a coffee at Newport Pagnell services using little else but sleek sentences and a gentle sigh of pleasure. However, when it's not happening that sigh is easily replaced by a groan, as the braking distance of similes and adjectives result in being tailgated so dangerously that you're afraid to pull over; and even if you do there's no parking spaces.

I discovered my new and supposedly exciting characters were failing to live up to expectations. They had all the motivation of seasoned supporting actors on two-dimensional sets of Westerns. I wonder if it might be like that moment when you buy the house that you've sighed over for all those years. You move in and sit outside to watch passers-by admiring your frontage and it occurs to you that they now have all your dreams. Mind you, I'd certainly like the opportunity to find that out from the upper deck of a beachfront house in Leigh-on-Sea.

But back to writer's block. I suspect that writer's block is actually a euphemism for depression; when you lose grip of yourself and the spark has gone. Despite Bukowski's encouragement, no one wants to read about a depressed writer. It is a road paved by barflies and broken men and women stroking cats. Being depressed is like having 40-years' worth of memory displaced by a morning so low you may as well lie beneath the carpet. Some writers feel only as good as their last line. The trick is akin to driving in the snow. You must plough on. Maintain momentum. If you stop, you might freeze to death.

The hardest part is struggling with the idea. Is it you, or the idea? If you're not excited by it then why would anyone else be? They're unlikely to see something in it that you missed. Mind you, if you can't take in the positive reviews then what's the point. I'm sure you can write another novel. You may not be climbing but the summit is still there. We often spend time in the clouds. It's seen as a good thing, but when you can't see the path ahead, it feels dangerous and unsafe. Go carefully; but keep moving as Hunter S Thompson advised. It's one step at a time, or perhaps there's a wool loom in need of repair; call it research.

163

Never give up on Creativity.

Always stop with a victory. - Robert Greene, The 48 Laws of Power

What is it with starting things? We are constantly told how we should be doing more. And advice in leading fuller, more enriched lives invariably concerns starting something. Apart from cars. If they're not starting you may as well buy a new one, cars are like toasters these days, if you could buy a £16,000 toaster on finance.

The urge to start something frequently outweighs the desire to finish anything. Starting things means walking giddy on the hope; it's being thrilled by the concept that hasn't failed to be captured yet. Eventually projects and ideas are finished, but there's definitely more plans started than finished.

Every journey starts with a single step - before returning home for your phone charger - but where should we stop? A journey may start on the London Underground's Circle Line, but if you don't get off, you're just going around in circles. Well, in fact you're not because it doesn't really make the shape of a circle. It's shape more accurately replicates that of a small wading bird, but no one's ever going to recommend you get the small wading bird line to Sloane Square. In fact, at closer inspection the Circle Line is the shape of Sandpiper, which now sounds like the best line on the entire network. It would also demand the phrase 'I'm going around in bloody Sandpipers' when frustrated.

Anyway, when to stop, as I just failed to. We know all about starting, but how about stopping something. Giving it up. There came a time when spooning three tablespoons of sugar into a mug of tea became socially unacceptable. Even builders appear to have reduced their sugars to two. One even had his own sweeteners, although sadly not mounted on his utility belt. It was a sad sight, those little dots of sucralose making as much of a splash in the tea as his daily calorie intake. I noticed he didn't finish it though.

From having children, to ordering tequila, there's as much art in knowing when to stop as there is in starting any project. Knowing when to stop editing a book is *definitely* an art; if you're not watchful then editing can become simply re-establishing what was previously removed, which is going around in serious sandpipers.

These days, from Facebook spats, to Twitter face masks, to sanctimonious cyclists, to the seemingly endless need to feel offended, no one seems to know when to stop. Most TV series suffer from this, even the highly rated *Peaky Blinders*, the recent series of which seems to exclusively involve Tommy Shelby wearing increasingly huge Baker-boy tweed caps and looking moodily on as rival gangs clash in a slo-mo videos to coarsely authentic rock music. It's all very pretty to look at, until you realise that, bar the tailoring, it all stopped making sense several seasons ago.

It can be the same with writing, and other creative endeavours. We are as sensitive to negative feedback as we are in need of approval and praise. Plenty of writers give up on novels, which is the sort of news sending optimists into a tailspin, as they desperately flick through positive-thinking prompt cards to counter such defeatist negativity. Sometimes it might be a very good idea; it cuts the bad reviews off at the pass.

As we've established, bad reviews can hurt. After attempting to drown himself in the sea Evelyn Waugh burned *The Temple at Thatch*, his unpublished first novel in 1925, after a friend gave it a bad review. His drowning attempt went just as poorly. He got stung by a jellyfish and presumably changing his mind. There's an important lesson to be learnt here. Harper Lee famously never followed up *To Kill a Mockingbird*, until 55 years later when her *Go Set a Watchman* was published, which was effectively a first draft of the first book. She had said after her huge success

165

that 'When you're at the top there's only one way to go.' Her publisher should have paid heed, as it does nothing to enhance her reputation, and she died in the year following its publication.

Authors are sometimes correct in giving up. Truman Capote's follow up to *In Cold Blood* was *Answered Prayers*, which was posthumously published, and described by critics as: 'it was never finished because it wasn't going anywhere.' It had also upset so many of his friends that it propelled him into depression. If only he'd left it in the drawer, or even better, his head.

Writing is a difficult beast, but unlike the weight of a rhino, the absence of words can crush a writer, but beware of creativity for the sake of protecting yourself from not being creative. This might sound rather meta, but Richard Price abandoned his 1970s novel *Home Fires* because its impetus was panic about not having a novel to work on. It's all very well banging away in the shed, but if you're not making anything then it is pointless.

So, when do you give up? Writing a novel is a big ask, which often appears to have no answer. You are making such tiny steps that they feel unrelated to any progression. Perhaps this is simply hitting the wall, as marathon runners put it; when you've had enough of slipping across ankle-deep plastic bottles and want to lie down under some kitchen foil. Is it something to overcome, or to embrace? No one can tell you, although there is the sense that Harper Lee and Capote's instinct told them to abandon their books, but under pressure from their publishers they did not.

Abandoned novels can be a crucial part of the process. John Updike wrote two thirds of the unpublished *Willow*, before abandoning it, although it bled into subsequent books. However, he did return to its themes in subsequent short stories. 'A writer - I suppose any artist - will tackle something again and again until he sort of does it.' He said, adding that the abandoned *Willow* was not a wasted effort, simply a premature one.

Starting something is celebrated, while stopping is heart-breaking and frowned upon. It's your call, make it. But it's unlikely to be wasted time. Every tiny moment of our lives impacts upon us like dust on an old piano; you don't notice it happening but eventually it will bury us. Pull up the lid and play. And if it means occasionally throwing yourself in the sea then at least it cleans the dust off; just check for jellyfish first.

How to write a short story

A short story must have a single mood and every sentence must build towards it. Edgar Allan Poe.

Short stories? Well, they must be so easy. They take twenty minutes to read and surely not much more time to write. It's nothing like the Himalayan trek without Sherpas, supplies or basic knowledge of mountaineering of the Great Novel. No need to be worrying about 500-page story arcs, or where you're going to find all those words. You don't waste time getting the angle of trees shadows at 4pm correct, you simply get to the point. Writing short stories also avoids batting off enquiries from family members as to why you haven't finished yet. Just sit down, knock one out, and then start writing (boom).

Short stories used to be the scaffold to any fledgling literary career. They are snappy, cool, quick, concise, well-balanced and elegant. Other than these things what's not to like. We live in a time-poor age, although that could be avoided by not checking our phones with the regularity of nuclear reactor operators. I swear some apps are wired up to life support systems: stop clicking and you die. I don't watch Black Mirror, but I'm guessing this has been covered.

Maybe it's because there's no money in short stories. As boxing promoter Eddie Hearn says, if you sit a fighter down to decide where to fight and say 'there's £30million in England or £60million in the Middle East, it's a very short conversation.' Where magazines would once dine Fitzgerald for more content, they can now make do with opinion columns or a fashion shoot.

Anyway, although too often better suited for weighing down tarpaulins in tropical storms than reading, the weighty, important tome of a novel prevail against the odds. However, the masters of the short story remain in such high regard that they are mentioned in the similar hushed tones used to name drug dealers: Joyce, Carver, Wilde, Chekhov, Hemingway, Fitzgerald,

168

Wodehouse. Damn it, they can even dispense with their Christian names. You're well-advised to avoid reading these authors if you want to start writing shorts. Perfection is a good thing to aim for, but it is best keep it out of eyesight, not only off the desk but in the other room. Under the bed. In a box.

Perhaps the hardest thing with short stories is that it's harder to find excuses for not finishing them. You write one, and then realise you'll need to write another five to make a compendium, and then find another great title. It's basically tricking yourself into writing a novel, which was totally not the idea.

That's not to say there is no initial excitement of writing a short story. After all, what could be more thrilling than sitting down. The plan of nailing words tighter than submarine rivets might last for as long as the opening line, but the precision soon gives way to random words, a desire to shoehorn in the word 'supine', notes of disconnected dialogue and a well-developed rider for backstage requests following signings, should it sell a million copies. This sketch of an idea bears as much semblance to your original exciting spark of inspiration as a square of burnt grass does to barbecued ribs. It will then sit on your hard drive under some forgotten file name until you get a new laptop. Like any barfly, and most writers, I've started more stories than I have finished; my laptop is full of homeless stories and opening paragraphs. I guess you could join them all together in some experimental attempt to win the Man Booker Prize.

Cut away:

Once the Thames falls out of the tourists' sight at the bend that curves around the north Greenwich peninsula, the river grows rather unruly. Now, beneath lockdown skies, herons strut the foreshore and willow trees have taken hold in the embankment walls, through which Canary Wharf's skyscrapers stand bold. Even at this distance you know the offices are empty. Phones sit silent and no desks are festooned with Christmas decorations. Stairwells howl with lost wind and pubs seem hollow without the potential that drinkers bring to the booze.

The river meanwhile is no longer the moody teenager of upstream, but rather an old man who no longer cares what anyone thinks. We pass the industrial sand works and the O2, and London is gone. There's the Silvertown sugar factory, and the Woolwich ferry clanks furiously as it wrestles with the unrelenting tide. An older couple stop to sit on a partly vandalised bench to share tea from a thermos.

The carcass of a ship sits offshore. The pool table of the recreation room gathers dust, what is a ship without sailors or a world without people? Is there Life without Living.

The Importance of Reading books

Life never happens in chapters, no matter how often we walk around at pertinent moments holding up numbers on large cards like a ring girl. Instead, life occurs in a largely forgettable surge of loitering, mealtimes and losing stuff; of shouting at the radio, deaths, births and vocal opinions. The ideal for living slips perpetually out of our reach. We should be used to it by now, but I'm unsure we ever make our peace with discrepancy between what we want life to be and what it actually is. A bit like those disappointing novels.

I'm aware that this chapter appears to be advertising the bookshop in Reading, Berkshire's leading commuter town, but it occurred to me that it's all very well banging on about how to best write books, but if people don't know how to read the blasted things it all feels like a waste of time. We have covered how to buy them, unless you skipped that bit, but reading them is an art form itself. In a modern world of boxsets, bagels and lockdowns it is a wonder anyone is reading, yet the literary world remains a safe place for anyone seeking refuge and peace, excitement and intrigue. Although if publishing houses have their woke way this might be about to end. It was encouraging to find that surveys revealed people to be reading more during the lockdowns, although if the only recourse to increasing people's reading is to lock them in their houses then we still have a long way to go.

If we didn't read, we'd be unable to forget where we were reading something interesting that we can no longer remember. People keep books on shelves not to reread them, but to be reminded that they have read them, so they don't buy them again, even if all they can recall is that it featured a donkey at some point in chapter six, which in a re-read reveals itself to be a moped in chapter eleven. Books are also obviously a fine, albeit cliched, backdrop to Zoom calls, so long as people don't zoom in to discover your interest in Third Reich tailors.

Just as other people's laundry smells better than your own, books in bookshops always appear more appealing than the one you're reading, which means buying it. The real challenge is to finish the one you're reading, or at least to not allow your current book to see that it's being cheated on.

The art to reading is tenfold:

1) Never leave home without a book or it will ruin your day. This might mean reaching the train station and needing to return home despite already being late, but even that is better than being bookless. It's important to have a book even if you fail to read it due to being addicted to your phone. It's security, and by that I don't mean you can wallop an aggressor over the head with it. The likelihood of finding yourself in a queue is quadrupled if you have nothing to read on your person. And if you get arrested, unlike your phone, they're unlikely to take your book.

2) However, connected to this is that in fact you can kill someone with a book. This can be metaphorically, via bold delivery of the facts to counter their arguments, or if you are John Wick you can actually kill someone with a book. I think Jason Bourne also took on an assailant with a book, so I could just rest my case for reading here. Or was it a potato peeler? Anyway, you can't kill anyone with your phone, or even a kindle, not that I've tried.

3) Always read to the end of a chapter. This doesn't work if like *The Collector* by John Fowles as the novel has no chapters. But it does push you forward. I like books where writers inadvertently make you tired before falling asleep. These days this can range between a quarter and half a page. I can hear bookworms already agitating at this blasphemy. They will start a book and like a goat eats a whole basket of laundry regardless of how it smells, will have finished it by lunchtime.

4) Find somewhere comfy. Reading is as much about your body shape in a bean bag as it is about the book.

5) Remember that reading is a strong look. I realised a long time ago that someone reading a book is automatically at least 15% more attractive than someone playing Pokemon Go. I didn't exactly take books on dates, but I sure as hell talked about them. There was always a novel sticking out of my pocket. Yes people, it was a novel. Try discussing how much fruit you stacked up on Candy Crush during a date and see how far you get.

6) Another made up fact is that reading makes you 50% more intelligent, but of course this has to be the case. University libraries are not shelved with SNES and PlayStation games or fidget spinners and mobile phones, but with books. Books full of stuff to improve, or even agitate your life.

7) The battery on your book never dies, so you are safe; it will never let you down leaving you with nothing to read but the back of a bus or train headrest.

8) You are never lonely. Not only do books keep you company, but they also provoke conversation. Most book readers cannot resist joining in on another conversation about a book, particularly if it sounds good.

9) A really great thing about reading is that someone else does research for you. Thanks to Graeme Macrae Burnet's *His Bloody Project* I knew everything there was to know about Scottish peat Crofters, for about four weeks. I've forgotten it all since, but then Burnet has probably forgotten it too.

10 I hate no. 10. It's there to make lists numerically pleasing. It is the desperate sound of a travelling entertainer with his matchstick animal show, mesmerising crowds with his models of snakes, worms and giraffe necks, oblivious to the children who want him to stop so they can have an ice cream and the party bag. But there is one more important point about reading: it puts your head in a different space. The world with all of its complexity

sits within inches of your face. And you have time to consider it. What more could you ask?

Achievement.

I have been writing whatever current novel I'm working on for longer than I care to admit without heavy sedatives. The Magna Carta had more recent redrafts. I recently asked a Costa prize winning novelist how long it had taken him to complete his novel. Seeing him hesitate, I asked for the truth; so that I might feel better about mine. With a shudder, he mumbled 'about nine years.' This made me feel a lot better. Now he has all the time in the world to write a follow up, so he's probably hyperventilating in a dark room over-thinking how he did it the first time. Or teaching creative writing somewhere.

Achievement is life's rainbow; it keeps moving. You might bask in the glow of having actually found your house keys without requiring help, but the sense of success is fleeting. It's human nature. Not content with bubbling away in some primordial sea, humans crawled onto land and started inventing the hole-punch and hotel chains, before eyeing the stars and deciding the moon needed footprints. We are discontents. It's why we admire dogs and pigs so much; they know which side their bread is buttered, and if it's not buttered, well, there's still bread, and if there's no bread, there's always mud, or a walk, or sleep until there is. They chase sticks, not contentment; they just lie down on that.

My literary achievements so far have involved having once sent the correct draft to a literary agent and publishing two novels with a publisher evidently keener on signing novels up than promoting them. It's probably no coincidence that they have stopped their literary arm to concentrate on self-help books and business manuals. Perhaps they know something I don't, but I always sensed they had walked too far into the woods holding the map upside down. I said nothing, as no publisher wants to be told they aren't doing enough for their writers, and although I suspect that's a familiar mating call in the industry. My imprint discovered new lows in neglecting promotion. God, I sound embittered. I'm not. I was delighted to be in print, and I'm grateful I was signed, but their involvement made riverside fishermen appear proactive.

If achievement is habitually sitting across a café table from your own bag, then I've made it, but losing my first agent was the biggest blow. It felt like discovering your ticket is invalid at an airport check-in. But after I lost my editing grew ruthless, I took out all the jokes, which pretty much only left punctuation and wing-bats, but it led to a second agent. And after I lost them, I rewrote the jokes and put them back in. And that got me the publisher. You see how it works? If you do then please let me know. Twenty years in and I'm none the wiser. All I really know is how much I enjoy writing, sometimes. I've certainly lost touch with why I wanted to be a novelist in the first place.

Like someone exclusively drinking raspberry Slush Puppy as a child and wondering why they're blue, I was as fully responsible for my own predicament as anyone driving without a steering wheel can be. Why I wanted to be a novelist is probably best left to my therapist, but I was basically chasing the dream of a teenager. Teenagers are those things that dislike eye contact, end every sentence with a high-rise tilt (like, why the fuck are you doing that?) and change identity far quicker than they can empty their room of mouldy tea mugs and plates of toast crumbs.

I'm basically following career advice from my teenage self, who's only life skill was miming the guitar solo to Whitesnake's *Is this love?* and being unable to stagger out of bed without looking like he'd been shot. But now it's too late. My novel is effectively a mental shed I disappear to when there aren't dinner guests, and when there are dinner guests, when there's nothing on TV, and when there is. It's an escape, and one I'm unable to give up. Getting published simply vindicates the years spent sitting opposite my bag in cafes, hotels and pubs around the world, but it did not bring peace. I wanted a better publisher. One who might ring me as opposed to the other way round. And then there's the worry that two novels were a fluke, and I can't follow them up.

Just Keep Walking.

My grandmother started walking five miles a day when she was sixty. She's ninety-seven now and we don't know where the hell she is. - Ellen De Generes.

BBC radio is currently hooked on programmes about walking, which can only be assumed were recorded at a time of year when rambling is a good idea, as opposed to February where the pull of the nearest pub or cafe marks the furthest reach of any expedition, unless you enjoy swearing at the rain.

It was news to me that writers even like walking. I thought they considered it an extreme sport without the access to energy drinks. But it's good to hear that a harmless pastime is now identified as another symptom caused by compulsion to join words together. I can see why writers might enjoy walking, like skydiving it's hard to write while you're doing it, yet it is more accessible. Or is it? Walking in the 1970s was popular because it was preferable to sitting in a Ford Cortina, where arctic blasts at speeds above 20mph cut through all occupants from the rust-holed bodywork with the ease of a category 5 gale. It didn't matter how hard you gripped the thermos flask; it was the sort of cold that you take to your grave to warm up; besides, the thermos negatively impacted the ability to steer. The occupants were happy to do anything on arrival anywhere, including walking, than endure another second of bad suspension and broken seatbelts.

Contrary to popular belief people walk more in the city than the countryside. I have no evidence for this beyond the fact that rural folk drive to their gym. However, I can't believe the flow of people trampling across London Bridge into the City every morning are writers. I bloody hope not. I used to be special. I prefer not to believe they consider it as crucial reverie cueing up a day spent burning their fingertips in a haze of creative electricity. Likelihood is they're all too preoccupied with why they didn't stop at the Pound shop at the weekend to buy forks

178

for the staff kitchen; the absence of which will make them furious at lunchtime.

I've always liked walking. The lunchtime stroll made going into work worthwhile; I fell upon (not in) forgotten Victorian squares, private parks, and canals I'd never have visited otherwise. As a social worker I preferred to avoid the pool car and walked everywhere. The car was always full of empty fried chicken buckets anyway. I'd often be filling in forms to apply for a support worker for my clients to help with losing weight. They should have simply accompanied me on my rounds. This was before podcasts; goodness knows what I was thinking about all the time. I was probably dreaming of how successful writers never had to walk anywhere.

Wordsworth was a passionate walker, but of course the pastime du jour is cycling, where middle age men can publicly slap their balls against leather without the expense of a Mistress, although there's so little change from £12, 000 for a Pinarello Dogma F12 Disc Sram Red eTap AXS 2020 that it's easy to see why even successful writers like Wordsworth might prefer to walk. Besides, a climb up a fell providing views across lake Windermere is surely preferable to staring at 'Dulwich Cycling Club' on the back of the next cyclist's lycra top, discussing the cost benefits of energy bars, and avoiding discarded plastic water bottles in the road.

So, what kind of walk is it that writers like? Generally, it is one on which loads of exciting things to write about happen, but seldom do. I'm sure their partners fully support such endeavours, so long as they grab some milk while they're out. Unless one lives overlooking a Regents Park, which needs no excuse to indulge its glinting eye with a leisurely stroll, a walk, like life, requires purpose.

Owning a dog is a good start, although letting it off the lead so it disappears, resulting in ineffectually shouting its name for twenty minutes, leaves you less popular than the pigeons, drunks and lovers. Those tutting the loudest will be fellow writers, and the drunks and lovers. PG Wodehouse had dogs, but they were Pekinese, so probably don't count. Cats are probably better suited to a writer; they're as equally self-obsessed, with little need for exercise, and the raised eyebrow of the most savage cynic.

Apparently Karl Ove Knausgaard didn't write a single line of prose in the time a dog was in his possession, for which some of us might grateful, and wish he had owned more. I have no issue with his writing, but it does need the sort of edit that the lack of writing due to canine distraction might be helpful with. Editing these days seems as passé as sun parasols.

It's important to remember at this point that American novelist Jane Smiley had a German shorthaired pointer, and Ian Fleming had several terriers presumably trained to not spill the 6pm martini at his Goldeneye villa. Let's also not forget Arthur C Clarke had a monkey, and STILL wrote over a dozen books. So much for monkey business. It would appear that writers prefer cats, or perhaps they are simply more disposed to taking photos of them and posting them on Instagram.

There was a time when I was getting so little writing done that owning a dog could have no impact upon it. I spend a lot of time alone, so considered it a good idea to be tripping over something. I'm aware this is precisely the sort of insane thing people say before the dog arrives to spend the next ten years swearing at it for persistently obstructing anywhere you wish to go. A dog is like a mythical beast that won't release you, albeit a rather stupid one. Mind you, I have no idea as to the average IQ of mythical beasts.

The dog arrived from an unusual source. People were falling over themselves during the first Lockdown of 2020 to buy a dog. They were a passport to walking the streets as our civil rights were robbed from beneath our noses. Yet an old pal needed a new home for their cockapoo. He could have sold it for thousands. Or I could have. It's such standard issue middle class dog these days that I wanted to call him Cliché, but he arrived ready-named. They failed to fully explain why they needed to offload him. I guessed it would reveal itself in time. I'm still waiting for him to attack redheads by the throat, or to bark incessantly at every passing airplane, of which there have been none in twelve months.

It hasn't taken me long to realise dogs enable listening to podcasts during the walkie times. They also literally drag you out of the house. You also get to regale other dog walkers, the only people interested, in amusing canine anecdotes, such as how Finn knocked himself out on some garden furniture while failing to catch a squirrel. See, it's a niche audience. A further perk has been how warm a dog keeps your feet warm and the central heating costs down.

Some Thoughts on Memory

The past beats inside me like a second heart. - John Banville, The Sea.

We struggle to recall so much of our lives, yet every stroke, blow and fall is recorded in the unconscious as easily as kitchen tables trace and recall the words of biros and knife cuts. We all dance to music that we cannot hear, yet have all the moves memorised like a chess master. We purr along our lives, idling like a classic Bugatti forgetting its grand tours and maximum speed, unaware of the innovation and engineering lying inches beneath the bodywork.

Memory is what makes us who we are and has been focus of medical studies throughout history. In the first century, Pliny the Elder described a man who fell off a roof and afterward could not remember his mother, neighbours, and friends. It is unclear if Pliny pushed him in the name of science, or if it was actually Pliny the Younger, whom the Elder had grown tired of introducing at the expense of his own social standing. The man had clearly damaged his hippocampus, where memories are made and stored. The Greeks named it after the seahorse it looked like, although it's more of a horseshoe, which either hadn't been invented at that point, or the discoverer had forgotten what they were called.

I have first-hand knowledge of an eight-year old's concept of time. 'Dad, I've made a new friend.' 'Oh, what's his name?'. 'Erm, I think I've forgotten.' With this level of early years recollection, it is little wonder we have forgotten most of it; when a newly forming brain can't even be sure if it has forgotten something or not. Our minds play tricks with memories. You remember your favourite blue jumper when you were ten? It was probably red, and a vest and actually belonged to someone else.

As surely as people driving camper vans invariably look baffled, we all potter around with a vague sense of purpose,

182

whilst having little idea of where we are, or what we're doing. It's been a long time since our routines were anchored to a cave and we died at thirty choking on indigestible gristle of mammoth. Now we have to plan for surviving childbirth and how to entertain ourselves after our bodies have given up. And all those memories. I wonder, if you had to keep one memory and loose the rest, which would you choose? I have one but it's best kept to myself, I think.

These days there's less need to remember much. No one has to admit forgetting British Leyland paint shades available as an option on a 1985 Austin Maestro, instead they can Google it. (Or even better Ecosia it – as they plant trees when you use it). Cars hold a lot of memories, not simply because we previously spent so much time in them; the average 0-60 statistics in the 1970s was 15 seconds. That's slow enough to run ahead and check the road is clear. My father insisted on driving at the speed of a tractor, and I vividly recall a tractor once overtaking us, which has to be life telling you that things need to speed up. He pretended not to notice, and instead pointed out an interesting hedgerow.

Things are named so they are not forgotten, and so that when you require something you can kindly ask someone to pass it. Naming stuff around us is what defines us. The problem is we started running out of names, and started calling car models after magicians, or foxes, or simply Up! Biologists and explorers spend a lot of time doing this, often naming newly discovered species after their own children. Victorian era family members were so plentiful that they seemed to exist to serve this exact purpose. It's unknown how many family rows were caused by a favoured child being used to name an impressive bird of prey, whilst younger siblings were used to commemorate the discovery of a new moth. Many biologists named species after themselves, but I guess waited until the return trip to Portsmouth to decide which was the most dramatic and deserving of the family name. There can be little worse than declaring a freshly discovered water Vole worthy of your name – affixed with the

Latin ending of ae – than it promptly being eaten by an unidentified sleekly manicured black panther that catches the sunlight as easily as the imagination, and yet still required a name.

I've often wondered if writers scribble, so they don't forget stuff. They are frequently found mumbling lines to themselves, while motioning to someone for pen and paper. Often, they subsequently look at the lines too valuable to forget with bewilderment as to why they appeared so crucial, but it won't prevent it from happening again. Making notes is essential to life, whether it be post-its, beer mats or an iPad. And to retain memories we need to make them, hopefully not displacing the best ones with the inane. So, onwards people, let's march into our lives and make more of whom we are, whilst making prestigious notes.

How near is the edge of the World?

Beyond the edge of the world there's a space where emptiness and substance neatly overlap, where past and future form a continuous, endless loop. And, hovering about, there are signs no one has ever read, chords no one has ever heard. - Haruki Murakami.

Sometimes the edge of the world is closer than you think. Sometimes you just have to get away. Turn the ignition key and put your foot down hard to the floor. You're free, your family estate car is a Jenson Interceptor, at least until the child's scooter collides with the rear window when you hit traffic on the south circular a few moments later.

London's too small sometimes. It doesn't matter where you live, your feet will walk the same circuit. We are all creatures of habit. Sometimes you need new sky to stretch into, even if for a few hours. Writers and dog owners understand this. On lonely stretches of riverbank or estuary mud there are walkers being ignored by their dogs lost in the bracken, or writers wrestling with invisible, half-written protagonists.

I needed a new scene for several reasons, and not just for my new novel. Following some shocking news, I found old emotions closer to the surface than my own skin. I felt rawer than a peeled orange. Where to go? Well, the Isle of Grain is background for my novel that is currently benefiting from research more vigorous than the 1960s NASA space program, so it was an easy decision. There are worst places than north Kent to be carried by a restless heart, and it's a change from windswept piers or being helped out of a city bar into an Uber.

There are also certain places that Time never even knew *to* forget, and the Isle of Grain is one of them. In fact, if Boris Johnson hadn't suggested it as location for a new London hub airport it's unlikely to have ever made headlines. There are few places more ill-suited to build an airport than wetlands of

185

salt marshes and mud-flats home to hundreds of thousands of wading birds and waterfowl. Bird strikes can ground planes even more effectively than drones or emotional support squirrels.

The Isle of Grain spreads itself as an afterthought of Kent with an almost nonchalant confidence; apparently unbothered that no one knows where it is. It's like the US rust belt only smaller and with more copies of *the Sun* propped on dashboards. Hopeful roundabouts shoot off dead-end exits, weed-cracked tarmac skirts abandoned power stations, and dilapidated barns crumple into flatlands. Rusting rail tracks lead to decommissioned power stations. Like abandoning the rashly agreed bowtie when hiring a tuxedo, security kiosks stand discarded beside collapsed perimeter fences to depots and decaying warehouses. A level crossing dissects an abandoned branch line, its tracks rusted, and once proud signage fades slowly in the winter sun.

London never felt more like another country. Mobile homes on driveways block the view from owners' actual homes, as they stare out through net curtains at the memory of last summer the same as the last. Amongst the barbed wire and field grass, along forgotten creeks where rotten boats wallow and storks' nest, there are traces that this virgin land has been walked before, by farmers and contractors, ramblers, twitchers and airport planners. Union flags hang slack in the wind and unkempt churchyards hold generations of the same surname.

If the Isle of Grain were a person, it would be the wise chap in the pub that no one notices until he has gone. And there are some pubs. In the Hogarth Arms, and with unnecessary professionalism, the bargirl struggles to spell my order of chicken Goujons on the order slip for the kitchen; after all she's the one cooking them. The landlord's building a fire, which goes out as a customer talking about contract landmine removal distracts him. He's a well-established barfly sipping a Guinness so slowly that he's likely to be there all day. Perhaps that's his plan. He's also explaining the intricacies of Malta's decline and its EU contributions. He's an army veteran, adjusting to civvies-

walk with slightly laboured familiarity; it's easy to tell he's more comfortable in fatigues and stripped out Land Rovers rattling with sand, grit and stubbed-out cigarettes. We are a long way from Islington. In the snug there's a small commemorative plaque to 'Barbara', who apparently 'always spoke her mind'. You can't help think no one's dared take it down in case she returns to give 'em an earful.

On the roads, articulated lorries charge into corners like its Druid's Bend at Brands Hatch with such ferocity that they rattle your teeth if you're standing there taking notes. (Yes, that was me). They know the roads far better than I do. Roadside trees are pruned; you can cut the prevailing wind from their branches, but you still know which way they'll always lean. A small airfield, better suited to smuggling guns into the country, and high profile extradites out, rolls its invitation to weeds and brambles across the flatlands.

And as I drive away, back to London, from the fallow fields and deserted beaches, the pylons and bridle paths, I can't help being pleased that such hinterlands exist. It may not serve as many people as an airport, and those residents it does are unlikely to appreciate its sense of purposelessness, but these lost places are important. They reflect the parts of us that are lost, but fail to find voice amongst the well-defined places, the jobs, the cliches, the noise and the fury, and the frantic dash in pursuit of identity and conformity. Sometimes you find something when there is nothing there.

How to survive change.

"Blue-bore", "blue-borie" - when the weather is gloomy or stormy, an opening in the clouds through which clear blue sky can be seen (Scots). Metaphorically, therefore, a glimpse of hope, a hint of the imminence of coming change. - Robert Macfarlane

When I began my idle thoughts, I never intended it to be a diary. To be honest it's hard to know my intention of regular blogging beyond growing a readership so large that I might then flog my own range of gold-plated trainers (guaranteed to burn twice as many calories). Instead, I appeared to have written a record, the not-so secret diary of Tom aged 40 something and three-quarters. Looking back, I can see how my sporadic and hopefully entertaining thoughts on why everyone is a twat, apart from me, actually mark my life, like sweets trailed behind Hansel and Gretel. Sometimes I wish someone was picking them up and eating them, but they're idle thoughts, so this isn't going to happen.

September is a month for looking back. I'm unsure why its claim is better justified than any other month, but still. Forget the forced celebrations of New Year, September was always the annual period of change. Countryside fields previously swaying with blankets of wheat now peppered with barren stubble; spent. It is the month in which spacious views emerge from between the leaf cover, while evenings tuck in more effectually than my old, oversized school shirt that I'd only grow into after Christmas.

In September change is in the air. December gets dark so early that it's impossible to see *what* is in the air, meanwhile nature has burrowed so deeply underground that it's hard to imagine it will ever emerge again. September is the month to live with these glorious dog days of summer; to reflect upon its July strength, as it now steps more carefully into the damp mud. It's the chance to live in those memories you were making for some distant future; the time in which you now find yourself.

But it's not just all about getting changed, it is also getting dressed. September is when you lose the ability to dress. In the morning you walk out of the house into the chilled North face of arctic winds and return into the house seemingly from a public sauna. You're either shivering in shorts and flip flops or wandering around London like a cloakroom searching for owners of its final unclaimed jacket, coat, jumper and a particularly ill-advised scarf. It's a moment of dissonance between where you think you are (dogdays summer) and where you actually are (cold fingered winter).

Unless you're a Lego figure no one is good with change. I once ate the same sandwich for six years at lunchtime. So that's not just once; that's every day. It was only a change of social work team that forced my hand and a review of the daily menu. I've not been to the Kennington Sandwich bar since, but just as café owners of the 60s would tense at the buzzing sound of vespas and motorbikes and imminent warring factions, I'm certain they'd automatically start making the usual panini with nothing more than an understanding nod. We all have our 'usual'. We tend towards the same people, the same books and films, avoiding all the significant change that we can. But we can't avoid it, and September reminds us of that. It's change that is forced upon us, like planning to renovate your bathroom, discovering the price of a La Rochelle cast-iron bateau bath, and opting for a shower instead.

I'm currently making changes to the start of a novel. I can safely write this, as regardless as to when you read this is its likely to be true. To be fair that's not narrowed down to September, it's what I'm doing if you ever ask me, at any time, day or night. My disbelief at prevailing mistakes in my manuscript is matched only by the strange surreal sense that someone else wrote it. Someone occasionally funnier than I often feel, and with a greater focus than the microscope I must have stashed somewhere.

189

So, how do we cope with change? We drink, we shag, we sleep, probably in that order. We exercise, we dive ankle deep into TV boxsets, we go to therapy, or shop for things we don't need or already have; anything familiar and the same. Yet the only unchanging certainty in life is change. Therapy understands this, it is a moving forward that characterises good mental being. As Kierkegaard wrote (when he didn't own a dog), 'an existing individual is constantly in process of becoming.' It's an astonishing idea to embrace, the one that implies the person you are with is not the same as they were yesterday. Therapy spends a lot of time consolidating yesterday with today. It makes it sound so easy, this sense of being robust enough to deal with the 'new and improved' *Super Noodles*. To just nod and not hark back to the past. That stability, instead of providing a boat of steadfast calm in a rambunctious world, can actually make you feel sick enough to fall over the side. But you do not break, you breakdown.

So, hold on tight. September is the drive home at midnight amidst memories of the swirl of summer lights and endless bonhomie that stuff the summers so full that one prays they will last the winter.

Keep busy

'Keep busy' someone once advised me. This is the sort of unsolicited advice people sling about like wellies at village fetes; with little thought as to where they might land. It's basically prescribed medication without knowing what the person is already taking. What if I'm already busy? However, it's not entirely bad advice. If you are busy it magnifies not being busy, which is one of life's great pleasures. It may not be Dionysian chaos, or Epicurus abandonment, but is pretty pleasant all the same. However, doing nothing when there is stuff to do is not the same as having nothing to do.

I'm not renowned for industriousness; as I've said before, writing a book doesn't *appear* to be doing much beyond quietly tapping your upper lip. My only reliability for years was avoiding real work like the moon avoids the sun. It's no coincidence that my greatest inspiration has been Jerome K Jerome and his beautiful musings on life, the universe and scones.

Beware the barrenness of a busy life, Socrates once said, which someone (probably himself) astutely wrote down before it was forgotten. Coming from someone who was a stonemason, hoplite foot soldier and later a founder of western philosophy, this is possibly a bit rich; much like Madonna advising people not to dance or to be ambitious. If you've ever seen a bust of Socrates, which might have been a self-portrait as he was skilled with stone, you'll probably think, 'there's a worried man looking like one of those turtles supporting the world while the other three pop off for some lunch'. He appears to have too much on his mind. As we all do. He looks like he could do with a lie down after throwing his western philosophy notes on the fire.

We are all so busy: working, driving, and playing angry birds, all too frequently at the same time. There appears to have been an unconscious internalisation of 'the devil finds work for idle hands' without a moment spent on looking at what alternative work options the horned chap might have to offer. Perhaps it's a hangover from the Victorian era, like geraniums and smoking.

Not that there's anything intrinsically wrong with being busy. We might pronounce it business, but the world is run on busyness, and the Western world has engineered suspension bridges, flying machines and the magazine racks rather than sit around and be accused of idleness. The industrial revolution might be boiled down to the fact that too many people didn't know what to do with their hands. The northern climates are too cold to be sitting around; if you stop moving things seize up.

With an instinctive dislike of work, writers often moan about having a novel to finish, but what's even more horrifying is finishing one. Working on a novel is pottering about amongst the wood shavings, unlabeled paint pots bearing no relation to paint shades in the house and spiders (unless you're Stephen King). 'What's a writer if they aren't writing anything?' the little voice whispers as you sit down with the TV to relax, before you give up trying to comprehend Dr. Who, and decide to do something else instead like flick through Netflix looking for something you might want to watch that looks slightly better than the previous thing you considered before going to bed.

But doing nothing is important. Retrenchment is crucial, as a traditional army, of which Socrates would have been familiar, needs time to rest after advancement, so do we. It is a chance to look at the territory conquered and to consider 'what is next?'. It's an opportunity to lean across large maps and push wooden horses across them with long sticks that it'd be rude to decline. In Australia, or New Holland (no prizes for guessing who called it that) aboriginal people would frustrate earlier settlers they were guiding by sitting down every few miles, when asked as to why, they replied 'to let our soul catch up.' Perhaps we could all learn from that without having to first colonise other countries and then die of scurvy. It may not get you out of doing DIY, but next time someone asks why you aren't doing anything, just say you're allowing your soul to catch up.

How to Write a Memoir.

I feel it is important to turn our lens upon the popular genre of the memoir. It's how I started with my teenage diary, and where I came closest to success with my memoir of social work. The logical conclusion to the current cultural authenticity police is that fiction, of any sort, risks cultural appropriation. So, perhaps to avoid the public thunder fuck across social media and debating societies, it might be best to focus on the memoir.

Rather than pursue high octane pursuits such as a week at an artist retreat, painting at a tea plantation in Sri Lanka, or being one of those people who tend to confuse public swimming pools as opportunity to socialise in the shallow end, perhaps consider your own story. The one that led you here, to reading these words, perhaps curious why you bothered, yet brought you here, nonetheless.

I had been chucking fictional plot ideas around with the industriousness of Paul Newman throwing a rubber ball at the wall in *Cool Hand Luke*, i.e. there's plenty of bounce but no stick. I was beginning to wonder what I should do, when I got a phone call. I know. One of those old fashioned wotsits, and I don't mean a cliché, I mean a phone, one that makes a consistent ringing noise other than a WhatsApp ping, a text ting or an Instagram bing; the sort of noise you'd forgotten your device made. I was unsure if I should answer by declaring where I lived and stating my phone number, as we once did in the (ahem) 80s. For once I was glad to have answered, as it was actually a proposition that I write a memoir about my time in mental health social work.

I was stunned. I was uncertain I had enough life experience to write a memoir, but my CV suggested otherwise: 18 years as a mental health social worker in South East London in which surely something happened. Well, I soon discovered it had, and some of this memoir has found its way into this book, because like the rag and bone men, writers like to waste nothing, well, nothing but time.

A word of warning here. In the publishing industry being 'interested' is still a very long indeed from book tours and soap-on-a-rope merchandise. It's the sort of interest reserved for momentary misguided consideration of buying a boat; the sort that despite genuine will not happen. In terms of the publishing house, what it means is that the person suggesting the idea hasn't actually told any of the other teams in the publishing house in case they laugh. It could not have happened at a worse time. I had given up all hope of writing, and it was a liberated place. I was no longer a writer. And it felt good. Yet, where was an offer on the warmest plate the publishing industry could offer.

With all the subtlety of arriving home more pissed than you are late, and entangling yourself with the bike in the hallway, I said 'no 'to the interest. The reason being that beyond recalling what I ate for lunch each day – that panini every lunchtime for five years, an order I still mumble in my sleep - I could barely remember a thing about my time in the NHS. It was like having been at a party without being able to recall a single word that was said, albeit a party you were paid to be at, with a generous public sector pension plan, with colleagues I didn't like, and no pens that worked. It's an odd place to work, like being inside a machine that everyone loves but you get oil and diesel all over your clothes and no one cares.

How do people write memoirs exactly? Do they make them up? Does anyone really remember anything? I mean you can ask two people who played golf together yesterday what happened, and both will answer differently, particularly if one is Donald Trump. You ask parents about your childhood and you're greeted by such blank faces that you question whether you're actually their offspring at all. Were they even there? The university years are lost in the booze-addled memories of scoring spliff with people you've not seen since, and it's hard to get character references for jobs from which you were sacked. And what makes a good story down the pub is suddenly rather flat on paper unless the reader is similarly drunk.

194

I thought it might be advisable to go through old diaries, although they are mainly rammed with the names of girls I never kissed and moaning about my Mum telling me to clean my room. It's not exactly exhilarating stuff; it's not rammed with first person reports regaling attacks on Damascus in 1917.

The hardest thing about being asked to write a book on my years as a Social Worker wasn't having blocked most of it from memory, (other than unexpected flashbacks of no teabags in the staff kitchens smelling invariably of oxtail soup), nor the overwhelming ingratitude for state interventions unrequested by the majority of clients, but the fact I took no notes. Or rather I did, but I don't have them. All my meticulous notes on drinking tea with people suffering from severe and enduring mental health problems are clogging up IT servers churning out enough CO_2 figure from the NHS proprietary data warehouses to floor an Extinction Rebellion at first puff.

Anyway, I thought what a wonderful idea. A writer who has survived the soul-destroying inadequacies of the public sector management system. I started writing. 10,000 words in and I spoke to the publishing house. 'Send it across' they said cheerfuly. I promised to send 'later', which of course took a week as I rewrote it. They even rang me to say that my proposal was to be discussed at the next editorial meeting with marketing. With Marketing! I mean this was the real deal. The market of medical memoirs was clearly buoyant, with *This Is Going to Hurt* by Adam Kay sitting immovably at the top of sales charts, and I was soon to join him.

It was a large publishing house, the sort with a name that even non-readers have heard of. The main aim of the book, I told them, was to entertain, but also to lift the curtain on the invisible work supporting people with mental health issues in society. It also intended to consider the challenge of respecting individual freedoms, while protecting the public and indeed the patients. It aims to look at the balancing of civil liberty with state

195

intervention and perhaps consider social services and the NHS with a rational and non-emotional eye.

I also looked at the risks that patients pose to themselves and to others, and the role of medication in treatment and its chemical strait jacket. It was also an opportunity to look at how much help is too much; at what point do patients become too dependent upon the state at the expense of their own independence and self-worth? Still with me?

The experience of years of rejection paid off. This time there were no wistful lists of summer holidays, nor measuring the driveway for size to accommodate American muscle cars. This time I put it out of mind and pretended it wasn't happening. Of course, this was part of the mystical plan to conversely make things more likely to happen, like ignoring the kettle on a camping stove when you're desperate for a mug of tea. I was close; the closest I'd been. I got an email, and I started to read: 'I've had the chance to discuss with colleagues, and I'm afraid I'm not going to be able to make you an offer. The general feeling was that although it is extremely well-written ...' I switched off. They added that the marketplace was already full of such memoirs and that a recent publication of their own – a nurse's memoir had not sold as well as hoped.

And this is why you should never write for the market. It's fickle. And publishing houses only really know what they were looking for when a competitor finds success with what they had probably already rejected a year prior.

I was rejected, but not dejected. You have to be bulletproof in this game. Memories are slippery companions; it can take the sight of 1970s National Express tour coach to refresh memories of holidays and the excitement of motorway services and Happy Eaters. I was in a familiar place. Here we go again I thought. Back to where it all started. The persistent desire to be a writer.

The Four Seasons

Weather is something writers have an enthusiasm for more often seen in ducks. Authors roll meteorological conditions lovingly between their fingers; they float in it and fondle any pressure gauge within reach; at least they do when they start. No character can leave their house without some rumination on the local climate. If they decline to outline their internal musings, then at least their clothes will be attending to the weather conditions in exhaustive detail. It's a tricky one. No reader gives much of a hoot about the weather, unless they are in it. Apart from wind that is.

Gales are always fabulous, sometimes because it means you can't hear the characters talk, but generally it's because they threaten. They are conflict personified. There's the most brilliant description of a hurricane in the prologue of *Scapegallows* by Carol Birch that the novel never fully recovers. Storms are the approaching calamity that novels used to revel in; whether it arrives or not is irrelevant. Unless you want meteorological conditions to stand centre stage then it is best to minimise it. Weather can however be useful to get the bat in the right position to strike the story in the optimum direction. You can edit it out later. No one sees the training of batsmen; all they care about is the home run. And the tea break.

Too much weather in your story might date it. The Victorians had no TV, so were understandably fascinated by minute variations in weather, but these days poetic descriptions of slushy Canadian sidewalks fail to stick in the face of smartphones. Weather can create a mood as easily as a Pinterest board; but you need to remember what season the characters are in, so they are dressed appropriately. You don't have them stripping off Aran wool sweaters at the picnic at which they were earlier sharing suntan lotion. Everyone knows what weather is, so are happy to see it through fresh eyes, if you have them. However, get the readers attention and like any meteorological conditions don't give them too much. So, here's a consideration of the four seasons.

Spring

Springtime seems a good place to start. I guess life started in the Spring, although the seven-day evangelists may beg to differ. Spring is hope eternal, but don't be fooled into thinking it starts with that first blooming bulb and the deluge of Instagram posts declaring spring has sprung as though the word original has been dropped from the dictionary. Such unoriginal thoughts are as slippery as spring.

Spring is the herbal tea of the seasons, the one which most easily seduces, yet offers empty promises. Like herbal infusion teas it is all smell and no taste. It knocks loudly enough on the front door to ensure that heavy overcoats and draught excluders are thrown away, before the front door needs leaning upon to shut against the arctic gales howling down the hallway. It's called a blackthorn winter, that spring-like period in early March which brings the blackthorn into flower, before the weather hurtles through a U-turn back to winter. Like a cute child, Spring knows exactly how little it needs to do to find love. It's the season in which you need to look at the temperature outside and not the month on the calendar inside. And we never learn. We take the Hawthorne winter as a personal affront.

Spring's arrival brings out smiles and hope, both of which turn to fixed shock at the realisation that winter doesn't quite let go for at least another three months. If you set a scene in Spring it will invariably be that week before summer arrives, at which point the previous three months of wearing ill-advisedly unsubstantial clothes, buying unused sunglasses and booking festivals will be immediately forgotten about; until next year.

Summer

As we look back and see
Our yesterdays entwine
The beauty and the truth
The summers of our youth
A-ha

Well, here's the easy one to love and not just because of its unflappable belief in itself; it is convinced of its love-ability like a Labrador convinced it's a lapdog. It is the posing and posturing RuPaul of the seasons: look at me, I'm what you've been waiting for. It's basically an 80s poodle-rock pop ballad set to blue skies and the thwack of green tennis balls arcing over the glow of strawberries. You might try to refuse its charms, but before you can say 'I'm never drinking again' you're drunk enough to be tripping over your own feet and saving comedy swimming inflatables in your online shopping basket.

It's not just full of hope like spring; summer is the suitor that not only implies good things, but it damn well promises them with the confidence of a field scorched by wildfire too. It sometimes even delivers (at least it used to). The summers of our youth stretched with the entitlement of Venetian Renaissance models on chaise lounges. They were the endless, airless days punctuated by bursts of irrepressible radio hits and sunbathing and hapless plans not yet sanded down by the coarse paper of reality. We teetered unknowingly on the cusp of adulthood, living out luminescent days; our feet pressed upon the emergent map of our life with the indelibility of paw prints in freshly laid concrete. Now those days whip by like, well, whippets on the scent, I guess.

Summer is the season people even talk about during the others. No one mentions winter in August; it's the mad aunt locked in the attic, never to be mentioned. But come January summer is spoken of in the hushed tone of a deity guaranteed to

199

descend from the black clouds swollen with rain with warmth and a magic caress.

Autumn.

The English are frequently accused of talking about the weather. That is if they can be interrupted about it, but there's just so much of the bloody stuff that it's hard not to. Unlike Australia for example, where weather forecasts in Coober Pedy have remained unchanged since the 1940s – they just press play on weather report recording after the farming news. If you listen carefully you can hear Anzacs returning from the war in the background. Besides, the English can't ask if it's teatime *all* the time. Well, we can, but the weather is a permanent option once you have that cuppa in hand.

October isn't a busy time of year. There are no fireworks or sleighs. Summer clothes cling on in full contradiction to the temperature facts. Shorts defy trousers, but barely. The weather is no longer as predictable as compasses at a magnet party. The temperature plays its usual tricks of appearing far colder from the window than it is outside. Not that this stops people from forgetting Autumn even exists, instead thinking Winter starts when Summer ends. They're the ones wearing enough clothes to stock a charity shop even before the bikini has been put away. When winter actually arrives, they'll have run out of clothes and be wearing sleeping bags beneath bear fur.

You know October has started when central heating is jacked up everywhere but your own house, mainly by people in T-shirts who clearly aren't paying the fuel bills. Trains, which clearly haven't been informed of Greta Thunberg, are hotter than they are in mid-summer. For passengers this means peeling off the layers of clothes to survive the walk to the station, which they clutch like the non-swimmer at a popular skinny dip. It's that or pretending it had been their plan to visibly sweat for six stops in a 28-tog scarf and jacket you could put poles in and camp for a week on the polar ice cap (if it's still there).

As the seasons change, there's so much to do. Replacing the duvet, buying a hat you will never wear, and digging out the jacket with so many pockets you'll need a Sat-Nav to find anything, apart from last year's lip balm, which is in every pocket of every jacket apart from the one you're wearing. There's even leaves to sweep up, that's if you enjoy pointless tasks and not waiting until they have all dropped. Then there's scooping out pumpkins, and living on pumpkin soup and stew for months, like the War never ended.

And then the clocks go back. Why is it that regardless as to how long we have been doing this, no one can quite work out when we get the extra hour or not? It's like the secret to eternal life that you left on the backseat of a minicab in an unlabeled bag. Perhaps, if we mess around with the clocks enough, we can live forever. We can blame George Hudson for daylight saving. He worked shifts and valued the light evenings so he could collect insects. It was implemented in 1916 throughout Europe, as it also helped to conserve coal needed for the war. But, it's not that hard to understand is it? (As he googles whether they go back or forward in Autumn and what it means). It basically results in children waking in the middle of the night, and in winter the gloom gathering before you've had your afternoon tea, which is a novelty for the first week, after which the rush hour takes on the characteristic of a blackout.

We go through this every year; our phones are smarter than us, and our foam mattresses have a better memory. Campaigners apparently want to scrap the daylight saving to reduce accidents. However, this might mean the sun would not rise until 10.00am in Scotland, where there's little need to add another reason for not wanting to leave your bed.

Autumn validates our constant moaning about the cold and darkness, but we should be grateful as the trees turn to russet, damp hangs in the air, and our hearts wallow in bittersweet reminisce of those sunnier days so recently passed. Let us not rush too quickly into the frosty arms of winter; let us breathe in the decay, and reflect upon how things always change, and another day will come.

Winter

There's a completely unknown 1991 song called *Winter* by a criminally unknown Glaswegian band called Love and Money:

Shine on, shine on / in the beauty of the storm, I wither

As with Summer, Winter has solid branding. It's got a clear identity with its face screwed up against a chill wind so cutting that it *has* to be personal. The only good time to meet winter is while wearing salopettes in the Alps in a warm cable car on the way to some cosy Alpine bar.

Winter is like the waiting room of seasons in which nothing appears to be happening. Everything is happening behind the scenes. That silent exploring of the thin line between rotting or hibernating is all you'll find if you dig. You spend most of winter either with a cold, developing one, or recovering from one. Coming down with illness takes so long that it lingers into becoming a way of being. Every breath is accompanied by a sniff and every search in your pocket insulated by hundreds of used tissues from forgotten sneezes. You're so bunged up you could suffocate yourself simply by closing your mouth. Prolonged kissing is ill-advisable, as fainting went out of fashion at the turn of the last century. To be fair kissing may have already gone that way too. Even sneezing sounds like 'a tissue'. We need to evolve our language, so sneezes extend their phrasing to include 'excuse me'. Meanwhile, people leap into hedgerows or busy traffic to avoid coronavirus.

Most people postpone the onset of winter by refusing to accept the deteriorating weather. They skip around in tennis whites and sandals as though a delay in digging out scarves and gloves alone might repel the north-easterly winds. Winter is full of fond memories: scratching your name in the ice on the inside of the bedroom window, whilst dreaming of double glazing, fighting for bum space with family on storage heaters that don't work, and being constantly told to close doors as a parent shivers in the draught of the house they bought. Summer is a long time ago to a rural mid-November.

Mind you, the London underground refuses to let go of Summer's stifling heat. Trains' thermostats appear to have two settings: OFF and FURNACE. For those accepting winter on the walk to the station find themselves sweating like a wrestler under too many layers, which become impossible to remove when squeezed in with an entire carriage of jumpers. The capacity of London's underground network is halved in winter thanks to layered clothing and jumper thickness. Some of the puffier jackets should require their own ticket.

From the viewpoint of summer, when you're arse deep in a paddling pool and paying your children to fan you with a newspaper, the concept of winter is appealing - oh, I can't wait for winter, I can wear my winter coat – is a favourite, as though it is a teenager's opportunity to ransack the family drinks cabinet for an evening. Winter seen from summer is all beer mats and bracing walks; all rosy cheeks and fires in the hearth. It's all inspiring hikes beneath blue skies across undulating Downs and heath. The beautiful editing of memory forgets the horizontal wind shooting icicles of air through your 'winter coat' with the ease of ball-bearings across a polished ballroom dance floor. It forgets that most conversation involves swearing at the cold rain when the sky looms heavier than a tombstone.

Talking of looming, Christmas of course overshadows winter like the Star Destroyer dwarfs the rebel spaceship at the start of *Star Wars*, but what happens once cheap tinsel has lost its shine?

The best place to be in winter is the countryside, where leaf-fall from the trees reveal entirely new views. At first glance bucolic winter might hold all the appeal of accompanying a year 3 school day trip on a hangover, but at closer glance there's elegance to the simplicity. There's so much less in winter, less to distract or steal the eye. It's all bare bones and branches, woodsmoke and grey. You won't last long without a pocket warmer, but it's surprisingly restorative, particularly if you're within walking distance of a pub after a walk in the weather, unless it's only got an outside toilet.

How to beat the Winter Blues.

So, how to beat those seasonal blues? And I don't mean Manchester City, although they are probably the least of Crystal Palace's worries. It's the time of year when weekend newspapers pack away features on 10 best bikinis, Get Fit Without Lifting a Finger, Top Ten things to do in Ibiza (and two to avoid) and How to Get a Beach Body by the Time you reach it From Your Hotel, and turn instead to life beneath the heavy skies. Winter is coming.

So, in the magnanimous spirit with which Scott Wildblood set up his speculative Life Assistance Agency, whilst failing to look up assistance in the dictionary, here are some idle considerations in how we might combat those seasonal blues.

Don't look at the internet. The first birthday greeting I got was from a German company offering me a £5 voucher after I bought a record stylus from them seven years ago. They're the only people who appeared to care. I whimpered as the rain hammered against the windows like a thousand relentless locusts searching for shelter. The second card was from my yoga studio, which makes it sound like I work there. If I worked there, I'd be sacked for non-attendance. The email didn't even offer me a free session like they used to. Do not engage with the internet. It's

204

full of mailing asking you to buy more of things you only needed to buy once.

Exercise. It might feel like wellies are now appropriate running gear but go out anyway. Any fool can run in the sun, but in lashing rain and wind, well, that's a whole new level of smugness last seen on the faces of writers at their own launch parties. The only higher level of smugness is running to your launch party, in the rain, in wellies, while holding the canapés. Actually, on reflection this just sounds like you're really poorly organised. Scrub that. Just exercise, it's nothing to do with the gym-bod, it clears the mind.

Boxsets. To be honest it was only months before the lockdowns that I was at a party wishing I was at home watching *the Man in the High Castle*. I was talking, I was listening, but I just wanted to be on my own with the alt-universe of Germany and Japan occupying the former USA in an uneasy truce. I'm unsure if it reveals more about me or the party. Apparently, according to a straw poll of one person, Philip K Dirk's book isn't that good, which means the screenplay has spun cotton into silk. Boxsets are modern phenomena that even Amazon are throwing sack-loads of their ill-earned cash at, almost as if it's some tax evasion dodge. It's certainly more enjoyable than a restaurant serving cardboard food while sex-trafficking from the kitchen. It also demands writers and book adaptations, so any writer denying they have one eye on the small screen whilst writing a book is probably lying. Mind you, during lockdowns it takes less than two seconds between a conversation starting and it informing the other person what you've watched on TV, frequently in enough detail to dispense needing to catch up.

Food - This is a tricky one. It's a thin line between eating comfort food and wallowing in it. Suet puddings might be a good idea for anyone keen to recreate the experience of sailors on the Arctic Convoys, but if you're going to be standing on the Central Line it is less so. You eat suet pudding and it's a matter of minutes before the doubt kicks in and you're asking strangers 'does my bum look big in this?' There's something too fleeting about food for it to beat the blues, but as my Mum used to say, 'a sausage casserole goes a long way.' Didn't we know it. It lasted a week.

Sex - We go from the tricky one to the downright controversial one. Sex is so complicated that it can make you feel a lot worse. The mindset of someone in the throes of passion is so far from rational thought that once you're released from its sordid imagination it's like looking at a foreign species, albeit one with more predilection for role-plays than corporate training days. Again, it's a great place to be, but you have to come back down to earth with a bump, and unless that's actually your fetish, it can actually worsen your mood.

Booze - We all know how terrible this stuff is because the government is constantly paying experts to tell us how we need to stop drinking it. Thankfully we're busy countering this with our own experts we met down the pub who reckon a few beers or wines are 'totally fine'. They probably said a lot more, but after the club, the cab ride home and a Doner kebab, you can't quite remember. The best thing about drinking is the day after the next day's hangover. It's like you've taken superhero pills and you're no longer walking as though the floor's making a loud noise. The less said about the hangover day the better, and very quietly.

Duvets - This needs no explaining. Sometimes the world is under there. Stay there, if you get the chance. Embrace it like it's a lost cousin, albeit one who's lost their skeletal system and replaced it with goose down. Are lost cousins even a thing? I always wanted cousins. They seemed to be friends you can't lose, and I was quite good at losing friends; I still am.

Hobbies - The above four sound like the contents of someone's rushed packing before imminent destruction of planet Earth. If any of those four options aren't in your hobbies, then finding one is essential before winter kicks in. Summer doesn't require hobbies. In the summer you can sit in the sun and it counts as an activity (at least in my book). In summertime just walking around commenting on what a lovely day it is can suffice. But Winter, well, get a hobby ASAP, before you're stuffing tissues into the doors' keyholes to stem arctic drafts and embracing the ironing. It can be from mud-larking to French Embroidery, to researching medieval naval knots to line dancing. It's important to note that what inspired my novels was a Saturday newspaper supplement describing the benefits of washing duvet covers on their own, unless you want to spend a day fishing out socks and pants.

Surfing - Apparently research has confirmed that surfing helps beat the blues. Well, for anyone who swims like a dog panicking in a canal (no names mentioned), this strikes me as utter nonsense. Not only does my local swimming pool not offer the sort of surf required, but you need camper vans covered with enough Live Life stickers that visibility is reduced by 60%. You're living dangerously simply driving to Cornwall, which I guess might distract you from being depressed. Once there you have to wear a wetsuit and strut down the beach with the arrogance of a traffic warden, albeit one with bleached hair like *Point Break* was an alternative to the King James bible to a monk. I know enough about myself to be confident that the best thing for my mental wellbeing is to stay as far away from surfing as possible, like in bed with a cup of tea.

Beware of tropes, ticks and tacks.

The underpinning of psychoanalysis is free associating. It reveals who you are with your guard down. And it's the same with writing, only you get to edit it before your analyst extracts the true meaning behind your words; if they're awake. We are reminded of how much material jostles inside our minds when awakening from a violent dream about abandoned oil rigs hosting the most abandoned party. You spend the day reeling from the hedonism as though it really happened, safe in the knowledge that you'll never be discovered, whilst ruing the fact that none of it actually happened; you fell but there's no bruise. Writing is the same as dreaming; you never know what might bubble up. It is the grit Indiana Jones throws to expose the invisible bridge after his leap of faith in *the Last Crusade*. All artistic endeavours are a leap of faith. You dive in with only the knowledge that you won't hit the bottom; you are safe on that front, but you are still required to swim.

That's not to say free associating is easy. It's hard enough in the consulting room, but through writing you soon discover your unconscious preoccupations. You might find that your metaphors always involve sheep, or that characters invariably stir their tea with their finger like a fading silver age film star. It's ok, this is bound to happen. We all have our stuff and it is bound to appear in big clumps like matted dog hair at the completion of your final edit. This is the tough bit. It's facing up to the limits of our imagination; how bound we are by ourselves. But that's ok. You're writing, so you can rewrite. You can change those sheep to goats, and then to alpaca woolen coats. Perhaps your character hates tea and prefers a shot of whiskey in their morning coffee like a site foreman tired of the grime of yesterday still beneath his nails.

It is through writing every day that forgotten conversations will re-emerge, and wisdom left on the night bus might sear through the morning. You may have no idea what lies beneath your rolling days as they gather no moss, yet sitting down to write throws light where you may not have expected it. The neglected aspect of writing is how revealing it is about the writer. It's intended for the reader, but initially it might be for you. The words are the threads to the jacket you wear without even knowing it.

We all lean to one corner and take a side; not just in football, but for walking, or where our hands sit on the steering wheel, even the side of the mouth for chewing. If you find a prevalence of Crombie suits in your characters make light of it. Perhaps a character copies another, to their continued annoyance. Perhaps it even leads to the gruesome final scene. You can't iron out all your biases, but as in therapy, you can grow more aware of them, and perhaps work with them. you can certainly learn to smile at them. They are you after all; and no one else. No one else will be writing with them. Yes, they're annoying, like too much company with the same person, which kind of defines writing; this is time with yourself. Be patient and be kind. Embrace your kinks, dents and tears, you can't push them away; just know they are there.

The End.

Generally, those two words draw things to a close, but not here. It strikes me as important that this book, as with all the best pop songs, has a coda. We all need a refrain. It's the drive home after wild swimming. It's the sex following a good date. It's the cigarette after sex. A friend with whom I no longer speak once corrected me on this. I'd been using the word decoda with such abandon that he finally corrected me. I was bruised, but grateful. An important lesson was learned that day: be willing to listen. How closely we listen of course depends upon how much truth we can tolerate. Humans aren't great with too much truth. We shy away from the ultimate truth, and this denial of death cascades throughout our lives. I was aware of this recently when I found myself on one hand upholding the fib of Father Christmas with my nine-year old, whilst simultaneously embracing the need for imminent sex education. I was tempted to follow my parents' example in this area, but I'm still waiting to see theirs; other than the existence of myself and my sister they remain remarkably silent in the area of procreation. Even now, in my forties, if I'm alone with my Dad, I still half expect the nervous clearing of a traditional gentleman's throat announcing a long-delayed father-to-son chat. Instead, he'll share his love of the 1856 type PB1/vii letter box and I'll smile inside. They don't make Edwardian gentlemen like they used to.

We learn everything we know along the way, most often via lessons we resist and embattle. The truths are there to embrace, their arms are held eternally open. It falls to us to catch the embrace, which we habitually decline. Writing is the same. Creativity can be a trip to anywhere: fame, fortune, discovery, or failure. It's a trip regardless as to where you end up. You may not enjoy it, but you can relish it.

An interview with Francis Ford Coppola revealed the sort of truth we avoid; he tells how he has compensated for his own lack of God-given talent he recognises in Spielberg and Roman Polanski through graft. Yes, work. Who wants to hear that? Yet, what magical advice: 'They can just do it.' He says, 'I have to work at it. But if you rewrite a script 100 times and make it one percent better each time, then it's eventually 100 per cent better than it would have been.' That sounds terrifying enough on paper, but who wants to sit around and rewrite a script 10 times, much less 100? Well, that unfortunately is the difference between a successful writer and a less successful one.

The reason for this coda is that while I hope this book has offered helpful writing advice, I also intended it to show the hard work required to complete a novel. I hope it also shows how unpredictable it can be; you're thrown around on the strings of disappointment and fulfilment like a test crash dummy. For every story of overnight success there are two hundred of slow burning disappointment. This is a book on writing that I hope provides some insight into what really happens. Writing 700 words is fine and makes you a writer, but it's stringing them together to make a story that makes you a novelist. You might find success, and I hope you do, but it's often by accident. That an audience even exists should come as much of a surprise as it did to Factory Records in Manchester, who were only doing things because they wanted to. You only discover what it is you want to do by doing it, as Tony Wilson used to say.

Essential parts of you remain neglected, but hopefully not forgotten. Don't stop at the gate, cross the field. Head further along the overgrown single-track lane to the boatyard, to where the sea flushes out the creeks twice daily and the pylons stretch the heavenly sky along the estuary. Be unafraid to discover what lies between; the old spaces crowded out by the new ones, the persistent whisper in the far branches of our mind. To reiterate: life doesn't happen in chapters. It doesn't even take place using coherent sentences. It occurs in a largely forgettable surge of hours, meals, shopping, losing things; of shouting at the radio and exercising or not. Life writes in sky-trails of births and deaths. The ideas you had of living slip forever out of reach. We should be accustomed to it by now, but I'm unsure we ever make peace with the discrepancy between what we want life to be and what it actually is. A novel is the same. As whoever it was attributed to said, good novels are not finished, but abandoned. Graham Greene was clear when he stated: 'the writer is doomed to live in an atmosphere of perpetual failure.' Any endeavour that provokes the word doom is probably best avoided, yet we strive on.

So, in the final words of advice from Lee Childs, whom I've never actually read, despite his repeated appearances throughout this book. His advice is good – perhaps for life itself: Write the slow bits fast and the fast bits slow. Good luck.

And finally:

There is one last thing to say about writing. People are often impressed by it. When I applied for my first job as a social worker it was through an agency, who asked me so few questions about my suitability for the job that I wondered why I had bothered with three years training. I asked her what the job might entail, which provoked much paper shuffling before she read from a job description most of which she clearly had as much understanding of as I had grasped of the computer programming languages while an IT recruitment consultant. I suggested it might be easier to email it to me, but she refused, citing it as a confidential document. Such pointless and obstructive behaviour showed in hindsight how I was truly entering the public sector. We confirmed a date for an interview with the forensic team manager and she sent me some advice on how to interview, which I ignored.

The security man pointed me past an impressive early Victorian gatehouse to the Forensic Community Mental Health Team. I was disappointed to find that Lambeth Hospital's architecture peaked at the gate. The team was housed in a car park that made the sort of makeshift building erected temporarily at the entrance to festivals where tickets are swapped for wristbands and indignant teenagers are searched for drugs look positively permanent.

I pressed the intercom, which crackled as though it had better things to do. Standing outside poorly connected door intercom systems would become something of a specialised subject over my next 18 years. At one point I considered mentioning my patience in these matters on my CV. It was finally answered, but for someone else, who swept past me like royalty. The first rule of door intercom club is to slipstream anyone who is allowed in. Now stood in a deserted corridor, I thanked her disinterested back as she walked away. I straightened one of the prints lining the wall, before wishing I hadn't. They all needed correcting and now looked wonkier. The inoffensive pictures were presumably intended to help sooth visitors, but even as a newbie I questioned the efficacy of ubiquitous balanced pebbles and liberal quantities of mauve to counter the dark paranoia of psychosis. They would become a familiar sight on the psychiatric wards of south London. I stood around, unsure of where to go.

With entertainment opportunities in the corridor waning, I overheard conversation from what transpired to be the main team room further down the corridor. There was a surprisingly thorough discussion about bananas. I pushed the door open and entered.

'I hate bananas. I hate the way they taste. I didn't used to, they look good -'

Before I could discover what disaster had struck to ruin the speaker's enjoyment of bananas, I smelled cigarettes as a large woman headed towards me.

'Excuse me,' I said. 'I'm here for the interview?'

She frowned, '*The* interview?'

'*An* interview. 'I corrected myself, as it crossed my mind that the temp position might be to cover her job. 'The team manager? 'I ventured.

'In there. 'She pointed at a brown laminate door, which I was immediately convinced led directly to the mid-1960s. I thanked her and knocked to a cheerful 'come in.'

It was my first Social Worker job interview that no amount of any three-year diploma could have prepared me for. I had brushed up my knowledge of the Social Work Core Competencies, on which I was more drilled than the North Sea. I was so well prepared for questions involving how I intended to apply 'social work ethical principles to guide professional practice' that I may have been mumbling it as I entered. However, I needn't have worried. The manager appeared so grateful for company that I wondered if he needed a social worker himself. He had greying hair and a poorly compiled suit in the unmistakably style of a public sector team manager.

'Hello, I'm Tom. For an interview? 'I announced, suddenly afraid that I had been let into the wrong building.

214

'Oh yes, for the locum role.'He invited me to sit down, while looking for what I feared was my CV. 'There should be three of me. The others couldn't make it.'

I sensed a grudging lack of surprise.

'You've just qualified?'he asked.

'Yes, just finished a placement in a residential support project for people with enduring mental health issues, where I used the social work ethical principles-'

My mind went blank, and thankfully, instead of pressing me for examples in how I had applied these principles, something on my CV caught his eye.

'I see you write?' he said.

I'll always look back fondly on this interview, one which focused on the Hobbies and Interests section of my CV like you always hoped interviews might. I was just grateful he hadn't picked up on Endurance Sports, which I had been advised by my sister to add in the hope it might represent inner steel, or something.

'I do.'I replied, wondering if I should lie and say, 'mainly practice social work reports.'

'That's amazing.' he said.

It was the finest feedback I'd ever had of a novel I was yet to start. 'Thank you.' I replied.

'I always wanted to write a book.' he added.

'It's never too late.' I said and he smiled.

'No, I guess not. The older you are, the more there is to write, right?' he paused, as though realising something. 'Did someone let you in?'

I nodded. 'Sort of.'

He looked at me and smiled. 'When can you start?'

That I could write, and evidently access locked buildings, which despite its absence from the Core Competencies would serve me well over my career. Grabbing the coattails not of Oxford illumini, but of postmen or janitors and slipping through already-closing doors undetected would become my superpower. It had also apparently secured my first job in the social work profession. The profession that led to many years of slowly

215

eroding motivation via ineffective management and the obsession with procedures at the expense of creative social interventions. My only means of survival, as it has been for so many, was writing. The lost title for my memoir was *Is There Anyone Home?* as this is what I spent eighteen years yelling through letter boxes. Not to mention the age-old shortcut to describing mental illness.

So, we come to a close. However, there's a final note. The sort of thing you might have expected to encounter earlier in a book on writing. I.e., How to write one.

The novel plan.

For those in a hurry, and I bet there's some of you wishing you'd been told about this earlier, here is a pretty standard outline of how to plan a novel. You can skip everything you have just read and just start here. Or just go on the internet. It's short and sweet and the closest this idly reflective guide to writing collides with actual advice. Other authors might give different tips and they might well be right. Check to see if they are more successful than me, if so then it's probably better guidance.

The three-act form is pretty established. It is what readers expect and what they want, well, you never know quite what readers want, they're frustrating like that, but this is the closest you'll get. The three-act structure is established enough to be missed if it's messed with.

The first act should account for about 20-25% of the length. The first act is the set up. In alternative parlance this might be called the hook. Readers need this, or they all swim downstream to other writers' juicy bait. Do not scrimp on bait. I'm sure there's a fisherman maxim covering this, but they're generally too miserable to share it with anyone. I've never understood fishing. You could spend the day staring at the river and swearing at boats without all the expensive and indecipherable equipment, but each to their own. Let's face it, fishermen they probably think writing is for losers and doesn't even get you out of the house. They might even be right.

Anyway, Act 1. The hook is basically a question; not any old question, but one the reader *needs* answered. The one they didn't even know they needed answering before they started. Do not mistake act 1 for a roll call of introductions. Allow these to spill out carelessly; do not bother with too many announcements. Too many characters and you're the teacher ineffectually calling Ferris Bueller's name. The intros can emerge later. Start with a question. Readers need to care and what people desire more than florid descriptions of the taxi driver's hair, is answers. And details of his hair product.

So, grip your character and make his response to something dictate the first plot point. It's major. Make it strong and true and land with the deadweight of a story to come. It tells us who they are. This is the conflict. It is the rupture that needs repairing. The question is shot skyward and explodes above us with a hundred more enquiries (if you like: they all require answering). There's no looking away now. We're plunged in.

We find ourselves propelled into the middle act, Act 2, which might be viewed as the centrepiece. The fulcrum. Here we hang the story up on its tightest hanger. It is an opportunity for the characters to respond to that major plot point.

The second half of the 2nd half is when your character gets their own grip on events. They start doing stuff. They are the horse with the spurs digging into its flanks. It cues up the explosive third act. By this point the reader is in the saddle with you. You might have no idea how low the branches are that you're heading for; all you know is that the trajectory is chosen. Have faith at this point.

It's not as easy as it sounds. We're surrounded by questions, but the mystery of where your own TV remote control has a limited audience. Just as real skies look unachievably spiritual after a rinse through photoshop, the exasperation between the lines will be lost in translation. Be unafraid of the creases. The edits iron it all out. And good luck. And be sure of the fact that there are truths. And remember: the only party in town is always the best party in town.

Finally, finally. What happened to the social worker?

Yes, it is the quiet ones you've got to watch. I learned that early on. To be fair I had not been listening in the weekly team meeting, but no one ever did, at least until they heard the team manager announce, 'allocation time'.

'Who's got space on their caseload?' she would ask, provoking the ten or so people in the room to start studying the floor with the intent of carpet quality assurance inspectors. It was a weekly dance of who made eye contact first. There were always new referrals, and the trick was to get an easy client. Of course, the risk was to volunteer too early and find the 'easier' client to be offered next, but of course if you held out for too long you may end up with a real handful; someone who will run you around the bend they had passed themselves a few years back. The one who will introduce you to police stations in the small hours and A&E at lunchtime.

The manager proceeded to present the client.

'He's a sixty-two year old married man.' she looked up, but there were no eyes from anyone. This always reminded me of attending an auction at which no one wants to buy anything. The team manager was hard to read, her emotionally state apparently ranging through varying degrees of pissed off and annoyed with little else in-between.

'He's been depressed for six months.'

'That's about as long as this meeting.' I whispered to Sarah, the Occupational Therapist, sitting beside me, before realising I had blinked.

'Thank you, Tom.' The sarcasm dripped across the room quicker even than the brown file already heading towards me.

'I can have a look at it.' I said like I had any choice.

Taking 'a look at it ended up in me being involved for eighteen months as Martin's social worker.

There was nothing on the IT system other than the GP referral letter. First onset of depression at an older age is rare, but not unheard of. I wrote him an appointment letter and a week later I went out into reception to greet him. I looked around, but there was no one either looking like, or answering to, Martin.

'Hi. I'm Val.' A woman introduced herself. 'I'm Martin's wife.'

She had the easy unflappable composure of a GP surgery receptionist. I liked her immediately. I led her to one of the rooms set aside for seeing clients.

'Thanks so much for agreeing to see him.'

I decided against admitting I actually hadn't. Martin had been foisted onto an already full caseload. 'That's okay. I hope I can help.' I said, looking around the room. I'm unsure why, as someone suffering from clinical depression is unlikely to be playing hide-and-seek. 'He's not here?'

'No. I can't get him out the flat. We live above the GP surgery. I'm the receptionist.'

"Oh, you *are* a receptionist.'

'Yes,' she frowned. 'It's becoming harder to live with. I mean *he* is. It's hard enough for him, but we've been married thirty years. He's a different man. I'm so pleased he's got a social worker. We've tried all the meds.' She proceeded to list the anti-depressants I had grown inadvertently familiar with sertraline, citalopram, fluoxetine. Names apparently created from randomly selected letters on *Countdown*. There was the first niggling on my part that I might not be able to help. It's a common experience in social care and never spoken about.

'Nothing works.' she said with a sigh deep enough to rattle the building. It occurred to me that she needed as much help as her husband.

I was unsure how home visits from a Social Worker might succeed where £billions of pharmaceutical research, traumatised laboratory rats and branded stationary that keeps the NHS stocked in pens had failed. I smiled encouragingly.

'I'll come round and see him.'

I saw her relief immediately.

'Oh, that would be great. Thank you.'

'I've not done anything yet.'

'It's all the support we need.'

220

It is a golden rule. Don't get people's hopes up. The number of times I had wished to lift a large case onto a client's coffee table and unpack a magic wand, which I might wave around erasing years of poverty, abusive parenting, low IQ, loneliness, poor social skills, psychotic voices and coffee stains, matched exactly the number of times I felt overwhelmed. The only solace was that I was never quite as overwhelmed as the client.

I saw Martin a week later. Val allowed me in the side door of the GP surgery and up the narrow staircase to their flat above.

'I'll leave you.' She said, exiting the room quicker than I'd left team meetings. A large potpourri on the table explained the room smelling like the floor of a mulled wine tasting, but not the gloom. It was darker than a crypt. Initially all I could discern was the lace of antimacassars on the chair backs. Martin was sitting in a chair with a gas fire on. I wondered if I'd stepped into the 1970s. There was a TV so old I wondered it received Channel 4. A number of china dogs were evenly spaced along a bookshelf.

'Hi. I'm Tom,' I said, sitting on a sofa that I was grateful to find was not peppered with hash burns as they so often were.

'Social worker?'

'Yes.' I confirmed, followed by a silence broken only by a bus ticking over at the bus stop outside. I looked out to see the number on its roof. 'How're you feeling? I asked him.

'Depressed.'

Even after years in the profession there's not much to say about depression. I tried a rebranding.

'How long have you been feeling low?'

'Six months.'

'Have you left the flat?'

He shook his head, and I decided to quit with the closed questions. The word flat sat between us like a black hole.

'When did you last leave?'

'Last week. To Tesco.'

We stared at the dollies on the coffee table for a moment. At least I did. I sensed him looking for the nearest cliff top. The silence was deafening. I had to say something. And sometimes

221

you have to bring all your training and experience to bear with a laser-guided focus, no messing around.

' So, you're feeling depressed?' I said.

'Actually, no.'

Well, this was progress, I thought. The silence ticked on; you don't often hear clocks, but it was all we had.

'Not depressed.' he repeated. 'I just want it to end.'

'You're suicidal?'

He nodded. 'But, I won't do it. I've got Val, but I do want to die. No one will miss me.'

'Won't Val miss you?'

'Well, I do deal with the marina.'

'Who's Marina? 'I was intent of grasping anything.

'Where we keep the boat.'

'Oh, you own a boat. 'I said. I hadn't expected that. The glimpse of a hobby; the glint of something other than the heavy dullness of depression, but it was fool's gold. 'You enjoy it?'

'Yeah. You have two good days with a boat. The day you buy it, 'he paused. 'And the day you sell it.'

'Ah. 'I felt the shutters rattle down. 'Something to look forward to then.'

I saw him the following week, and for the next few visits we sat there, amongst china dogs and listening to the buses outside.

'What did you buy in Tesco's?' I asked. It reminded of my first awkward date at sixteen when the conversation nosedived after we had discussed the restaurant's menu.

'Food.' He replied.

'You like food?' I couldn't believe I'd said it. The core competencies in social work might insist you empower clients to reach their full potential, but I was pretty certain that this was not achieved by asking grown men if they like food. He looked up from where he was staring, and I swear he almost smiled.

'Do I like food? Well, I used to.' He frowned at a memory. 'Ginger Nuts. I used to eat them with my Mum. He liked them.'

The following week I was buying lunch in Tesco and Ginger Nuts were on special offer. I sensed some higher hand at work; perhaps the Greek god of social work had grown as tired of the oppressive silences with Martin as we had. I bought a packet and took them with me on the next home visit. And I got a smile. It wasn't much, more of a hairline crack than a fissure, but I took it. And over the weeks I almost looked forward to our cup of tea and biscuit. I was due to start my training to be an AMHP, so had to handover my caseload to a colleague. I handed Martin to Sarah the OT. I passed her his brown file that was now thicker of notes that no one would read by an inch, and a packet of Ginger Nuts.

Farewell you all. And keep moving.

Acknowledgments

I'd like to thank everyone I've ever met.

Printed in Great Britain
by Amazon

36133486R00128